# Beyond

∞

# Reincarnation

## *About the Author*

**Joe H. Slate**, Ph.D. (Alabama), is a licensed psychologist and Emeritus Professor of Psychology at Athens State University. The U.S. Army and the Parapsychology Foundation of New York have funded his lab projects in parapsychology. His research led to the establishment of the Parapsychology Research Foundation. Dr. Slate has appeared on serveral radio and television shows, including *Strange Universe* and *Sightings*.

# Joe H. Slate, Ph.D.

# Beyond
∞
# Reincarnation

## Experience Your Past Lives
## & Lives Between Lives

Llewellyn Publications
Woodbury, Minnesota

First Edition
First Printing, 2005

Book design and format by Donna Burch
Cover art © Digital Stock and © Brand X Pictures
Cover design by Ellen Dahl
Photographs courtesy of Joe H. Slate

Llewellyn is a registered trademark of Llewellyn Worldwide, Ltd.

Library of Congress Cataloging-in-Publication Data
Slate, Joe H.
    Beyond reincarnation : experience your past lives & lives between lives / Joe Slate. —1st ed.
        p.   cm.
    Includes bibliographical references and index.
    ISBN 10: 0-7387-0714-7
    ISBN 13: 978-0-7387-0714-3
    1. Reincarnation. 2. Pre-existence. 3. Spiritualism. I. Title.

    BL515.S54 2005
    133.9'01'35—dc22                                        2005044992

Llewellyn Publications
A Division of Llewellyn Worldwide, Ltd.
2143 Wooddale Drive, Dept. 0-7387-0714-7
Woodbury, Minnesota 55125-2989, U.S.A.
www.llewellyn.com

Printed in the United States of America

## Also by Joe H. Slate, Ph.D.

*Astral Projection and Psychic Empowerment*

*Aura Energy for Health, Healing & Balance*

*Psychic Vampires*

*Rejuvenation*

This book is your passport to the exciting world of reincarnation and beyond. You're about to embark on a journey of a lifetime. There's no need to grab your suitcase—you'll be traveling light. All you need is a willingness to explore. You can now be whisked away into your past lifetimes and your life between them, even your earliest preexistence. So climb on board, and read on!

# Contents

# *Figures*

## Acknowledgements

I am deeply grateful to each individual whose support and encouragement made this book possible.

To the many research subjects who enthusiastically gave of their time and energies, I here express my sincerest appreciation. Also, to the students who served as laboratory assistants and technicians, I am especially grateful. They were always there when I needed them most. Although they do not appear visibly in this book, the results of their efforts are found throughout its pages.

I would like to thank my learned colleagues whose suggestions, criticisms, and encouragement helped bring this book to completion. They have my highest respect and admiration. I am especially indebted to Dr. Franklin Turney and Dr. Gene Chamberlain for their imaginative and insightful contributions. To Warren McLemore who assisted with the photography and to Ricky Pruitt who provided invaluable technical assistance, I express my sincerest thanks. To Isaac Dean and to my grandson Marc Slate, who contributed to every phase of this effort, I will always be grateful.

I wish to express my special thanks to the Parapsychology Research Foundation for its unwavering support and encouragement over the years. The Foundation's commitment to the search for new knowledge has been a source of inspiration that helped see me through this effort.

Finally, I owe an enormous debt of gratitude to Michael Maupin, my publisher's editor for this book, and to all the men and women of Llewellyn Worldwide for their ongoing guidance and encouragement. I hope this book reflects their highest hopes for bright new worlds of mind, body, and spirit.

# *Preface*

Here for the first time is a do-it-yourself guide for exploring the full scope of your past life. You can at last rediscover your past lifetimes, your life between them, and your preexistence. You can even get a glimpse into your future.

How is this possible? You have at your command all the required resources—master hypnotist, teacher, healer, and guide. Better than that, they exist within yourself—they are an integral part of you. All you need are the strategies required to access them and unleash their powers.

As a college professor and practicing psychologist, I can attest to the many benefits that my students and patients derive from self-discovery and self-reliance. Promoting autonomy in exploring your past life through workable, do-it-yourself strategies is the centerpiece of this book. With the exception of the Eye Blink Procedure, the strategies are based on studies conducted by the author under the auspices of Athens State College (now University) or the Parapsychology Research Foundation. The studies exist at present as unpublished technical reports and are cited throughout by Technical Report (TR) serial numbers.

With the strategies presented in the following pages, you can discover for yourself the spiritual essence of your being. You can finally experience the full magnitude of your existence. You can retrieve the past-life experiences that hold relevance for you in the here-and-now. You can uncover the unlimited resources available to you from the spirit realm, including your personal guides who are constantly poised to facilitate your growth. With these rich opportunities before us, who could ask for more?

Beginning now, you can embark on a new and exciting journey into your past life. The result? A newly empowered life of enlightenment, fulfillment, and joy!

*All the past is here, present to be tried.*
—HENRY DAVID THOREAU, JOURNAL

# 1

# INTRODUCTION

Have you ever wondered whether you have lived before and whether you will live again?

Have you ever thought about the full scope of your existence, from your most distant past to the present and beyond?

Have you considered the possibility that you preexisted before you were ever born into a mortal body?

Have you ever questioned whether there's an intelligence behind the universe, and if so, its relevance to you personally?

We've probably all pondered at one time or another these searching questions, only to conclude that there are no easy, ready-made answers. Figuring out the full scope and meaning of our existence is one of our greatest and most difficult challenges. That's what this book is all about.

Yet this book does not claim to have all the answers—they must come from within yourself. My primary purpose in writing this book is to inspire the search for new knowledge through workable, do-it-yourself strategies. Beyond that, it is my hope that this book will ignite within each of us a new commitment to use the knowledge gained for the greatest good.

The central focus of this book is on the endlessness of life within a four-dimensional spectrum:

1. Your preexistence or life before your first lifetime.

2. Your existence in each past lifetime.

3. Your existence between past lifetimes.

4. Your post existence or life following your last lifetime.

The term *past life* as used throughout this book typically denotes the totality of your past existence, including your preexistence and past lifetimes as well as your existence between past lifetimes.

The term *past lifetime* designates a particular lifetime of embodied consciousness in your past to include your first lifetime or incarnation and each lifetime or reincarnation thereafter.

*Discarnate existence* as used in this book designates a disembodied state of continued consciousness in the afterlife realm which is also referred to as the other side or spirit realm.

My treatment of these topics does not exclude the possibility of past-life existence in other realities or dimensions. In view of the vastness of the universe, and the possibility that our known universe is only one of many, it is conceivable that we have existed in other dimensions that remain either unknown or largely unknown to us. It is further conceivable that the theories and principles of contemporary science, at least in their conventional forms, simply do not apply to those dimensions. If, as Einstein observed, some dimensions are unknown to us, it would follow that the science required to explain them would likewise be unknown to us. Among my major research goals has been the development of new strategies that could uncover the unknown and help explain it.

My emphasis throughout this book is on the bi-directional endlessness of life. Incomprehensible though it may at first seem, only that which has no beginning can be endless. Your existence forever after your last lifetime must be counterbalanced by your existence forever before your first lifetime. You can't have one without the other. From that perspective, when we look backward into our past, we see no beginning; and when we look forward into our future, we see no ending. Your life's journey thus becomes forever continuous and immeasurable—it has neither starting point nor final destination. Simply put yet contrary to much conventional thought, your existence is from everlasting to everlasting.

This book steadfastly embraces a spiritual rather than secular worldview. It emphasizes the continuity of our evolvement within a flexible framework that acknowledges the spiritual nature of our being. We each exist within a cosmic scheme that is logical and orderly. It is a scheme that, like our own evolution, is neither rigid nor automatic but rather dynamic and on-going. It is not complete nor do we individually know all there is to know about it. Among this book's major goals is to promote a deeper understanding of that cosmic scheme and the magnificent totality of our existence within it—past, present, and future.

This book is based on the simple premise that the more we know about ourselves, including our past life, the more personally empowered we become in achieving our present life's goals. It is interesting to note that repeated studies of effective teaching have shown that the more teachers know about their students the more effective they are in guiding learning. It should come then as no great surprise that the more we know about ourselves the more effective we are in accelerating our growth and developing our highest potentials.

Wherever we are in our life's voyage, we are at any moment the sum total of our past, though we can scarcely comprehend its magnitude and magnificence. In one way or another, consciously or subconsciously, we bring with us into the present all our past experiences—from our preexistence to this present moment in time. Within that vast totality, we each become a never-ending work in progress.

Our past-life experiences remain forever with us for a purpose. But rather than being automatically available to us at the beginning of each lifetime, they challenge us to retrieve them and discover their relevance for ourselves. Only then can we integrate them into our present lifetime. It's through concentrated effort and self-discovery that we learn and grow. It's then that knowledge of the past becomes power for the present. It's then that we uncover totally new potentials to be realized and enjoyed. Once we discover them, our past-life achievements in particular can build feelings of worth and well-being. We become less constricted in our self-identity and more at one with the universe.

Even deeply painful experiences from our distant past life can be laden with amazing growth possibilities. Once we become aware of them through self-discovery, past-life disappointments can increase our capacity for flexibility and adaptation. Past-life suffering, whether mental or physical, can empower us with greater compassion for others who suffer. Past-life adversity can increase our resolve to overcome present-life obstacles. As we will later find, self-discovery of the past-life sources of our fears, anxieties, and conflicts can empower us to promptly overcome them.

Given the relevance of our past lifetimes, it is not surprising that many of us experience spontaneous glimpses into them. Among the examples are the past-life images that often surface during the dream experience and detailed past-life experiences that can spring forth during such altered states as hypnosis and meditation. Yet another very common example is déjà vu, which can often be explained as past-life residue. Each of these manifestations is a clear call to probe the depth of the past and discover its present relevance.

Even our experiences in the spirit realm between our lifetimes can emerge spontaneously to empower us in the present. Among the common examples are inspirational glimpses into the spirit world that emerge as "peak experiences." They often awaken between-lifetime memories that propel us forward with renewed insight and faith. Similarly, many of our dream experiences seem to recapitulate our between-lifetime interactions with loving spirit guides and teachers who remain with us to empower us in this lifetime. These experiences can be so profound that they literally alter our perceptions of the purpose and meaning of our lives.

In my practice as a psychologist and hypnotherapist, my subjects during hypnosis often experience spontaneous past-life regressions of important relevance to them in the present. Depressed or anxious subjects often re-discover a loving spirit guide from out of their past who had seen them through many difficult past-life situations. These spontaneous experiences often reconnected them to a spirit helper at a time they needed special support and reassurance.

Our regression studies repeatedly found that a loving presence from the other side often remained with us through several lifetimes to guide our growth (TR 7). Furthermore, like a trusted friend, they accompanied us at our transition into the afterlife where they continued to guide our development in the spirit realm. How comforting to know that we can experience in this lifetime the powerful presence of our spirit guides who have been with us over many lifetimes and who will remain with us in the afterlife!

Along another line, our studies found that subjects during hypnosis occasionally experienced a spontaneous phenomenon called hypnoproduction in which they demonstrated remarkable, complex skills which they had not acquired in their present lifetime. For instance, a graduate student who regressed to a past lifetime in Germany spoke fluently in German during hypnosis, a language he had not studied in this lifetime. Another subject during past-life regression discussed complicated scientific concepts using terms he had not acquired in his present lifetime (TR 12). Hypnoproduction can also include demonstrations during hypnosis of advanced musical and artistic skills that seem to be of past-life origin.

Each of these spontaneous past-life manifestations suggests a wondrous reserve of subconscious resources and inner potentials just waiting to be discovered. But for the most part, discovering your past-life experiences and retrieving past-life skills require deliberate, concentrated efforts. By discovering them for yourself, you will value them more highly, and you will better understand their current relevance. It follows that mastery of effective past-life regression strategies could access critical knowledge and even retrieve lost skills that otherwise would remain unavailable to us or else require years to acquire.

The basic goal of past-life probes is twofold: to acquire new knowledge and to use it for the greatest good, including your own evolvement as well as that of others. Here are a few examples of the potential benefits of past-life knowledge:

- Past-life knowledge can help satisfy the basic human need to know. Alienated from our past and devoid of its knowledge, we are like minnows darting erratically in a small country stream—enclosed, out of contact, disconnected. The unknown invites awareness and you possess the potential to experience it close up.

- Past-life knowledge can give new direction and balance to your life. As in mountain climbing, awareness of your past progress pushes you ever forward. It enlarges your perspective and steadies your resolve. Even past slips and falls can motivate you to try again.

- Past-life knowledge can build feelings of dignity and self-worth. You discover that you are a permanent citizen of the cosmos, not a flickering candle in the wind.

- Past-life knowledge promotes acceptance and understanding of others. Discovering that you were of another race, gender, or sexual orientation in a past life can increase your understanding and appreciation of others. Past-life enlightenment can eliminate bigotry, intolerance, and prejudice in whatever its form.

- Past-life knowledge has therapeutic value. It is one of the most powerful healing and rejuvenating agents known. Mental, physical, and spiritual well-being is at your fingertips.

- Past-life knowledge has many global implications. Given the magnitude of knowledge available through past-life probes, we become more compassionate of others and active in solving pressing global problems, such as hunger, poverty, disease, environmental pollution, conflict, and war. Possibly more than any other single factor, past-life knowledge can inspire us to help others and make the world a better place for all.

From our preexistence onward, life can be seen as an unfolding drama in which we play out many different roles. In one past lifetime, you may have been the star or the acclaimed hero who won the adoration of the masses. In another, you may have been the villain who was reviled and hated, even executed. In one past lifetime, you may have been fully dedicated and committed to your role. In another, you may have been a disengaged, passive spectator. In one past lifetime, you may have been a great leader who helped shape history. In another, you may have sought quiet refuge away from the noisy crowd. In one past lifetime you may have scaled the heights or made quantum leaps in your personal evolution. In another you may have struggled just to survive. Whatever the nature of your past life, your life's journey, when viewed in proper perspective, is forever forward.

Cosmic justice seems to be intricately woven into the broad fabric of our existence. When you recognize that adversity, reversal, struggle, and even tragedy are energized with tremendous growth potential, you can explore your past—and engage your future—with optimism and confidence. You will discover that where there was an imbalance of suffering and injustice in one past lifetime, joyous fulfillment almost always followed in the next. You will find that blocked growth in one past lifetime is a good predictor of quantum leaps in the next. As we will later see, our experiences between lifetimes often rearrange and integrate our past-life experiences, to include our setbacks and disappointments, in ways that orchestrate a totally new growth spiral.

Discovering the full landscape of your existence requires not only exploring your past, but more importantly, incorporating your findings into your present life. Clarifying your present-life view of your personal existence is the important first step in that critical process. I often encourage my students to examine their perceptions of their personal existence. Not surprisingly, their views vary widely; however, they are usually positive and optimistic. Here are a few examples.

- A business major: "I do not think of myself as a divine creation—I'm far from it! But there must be a creative intelligence of some kind behind the universe."

- A humanities major: "My life is constantly evolving in what I believe to be a higher plan, not only for me but for all of humanity. It's within that plan that I set goals and find direction."

- A psychology major: "Everything evolves. All you need is a starting point which can be accidental. I may be just an aberration in an accidental universe. Nevertheless, life is beautiful, and I'm glad to be alive."

- An undeclared major: "I'm still searching for meaning in my life. I don't know where that search will take me, but I'm open to the possibilities."

- A library science major: "I get meaning and fulfillment in life by helping others. I strongly believe there is a force for good in the universe. Beyond that, I believe that we sometimes overly complicate things, including our existence and the meaning of life."

Like my students, participants in my off-campus workshops express extensively diverse views concerning the nature and meaning of their existence. But compared to students, their views are more often edged with pessimism, with many of them questioning the meaning of their existence and the significance of their lives. Here are some examples.

- An interior designer (male, age 27): "I sometimes see my life as an accumulation of meaningless debris scattered across a wasteland. At other times, I'm more hopeful. Unfortunately, the world today seems to be spiraling downward, not upward."

- An attorney (female, age 32): "My life is like a comet streaking through time and space. Will it burn itself out? Probably. I only hope it will leave something behind, if nothing more than a trail of dust."

- A real estate manager (male, age 37): "My personal existence is something I seldom speculate on. I exist—that's all I know and maybe all I need to know. For what purpose do I exist? It seems useless to theorize about it."

- A building contractor (male, age 41): "I don't think we will ever know the full meaning and purpose of our existence. If we discover too much about ourselves, we may be disappointed with what we find. Sometimes, less is bet-ter—we have less to worry about."

• An English professor (female, age 49): "If we continue our search, I believe we will finally discover who we really are and what it means to exist. The truth will come, but only if we persist. I'm still searching."

• A department store manager (male, age 35): "We can never know the full truth of what it means to exist. My existence is a forever unfolding process, never to become an end prod-uct. There is no absolute truth and no final answers."

• A sociologist (female, age 45): "I'm still trying to figure out the purpose and meaning in my existence. There must be a reason why I am here at this place and time. I cannot con-ceive of going through this life indifferent and out-of-touch. Maybe that's why I am here—to more fully under-stand the scope and purpose of my existence."

• A personnel manager (male, age 51): "My search for mean-ing is an ongoing growth process, sometimes painful in and of itself. There are few guarantees in life—it's the uncertain-ties that push us forward."

• A high school teacher (female, age 30): "There are no fixed boundaries and no permanent solutions to life's dilemmas. The tattered culminations of past struggles are not end-ings—they are merely signals that mark our unsteady progress and jump-start a continuation of our endless search."

• A magazine editor (female, age 41): "I am whatever I decide to be. I am the author who writes my own life story. I shape my own destiny. Life demands my attention and action. The opportunities are before me. It's up to me to take command of them."

Many student and workshop respondents alike endorsed a spiritual worldview that recognized an intelligence somewhere in the universe. But ironically, not all of them accepted the spiritual nature of their own being. For instance, a mechanical engineering student noted, "The existence of a spiritual force in the universe does not necessarily mean that I am a spiritual being. I can be an intelligent part of a divine plan without being divine myself. My role may be to facilitate a plan greater than myself. I thus become a secular cog in a spiritual machine."

In an interesting reversal of that position, many respondents who held a more secular worldview were quick to note that they regarded themselves as spiritual beings. Along that line, a psychology student mused, "The universe is physical, I am spiritual. My existence therefore does not depend on the existence of the physical universe or an intelligence behind it. It's possible I existed as a spiritual being before the universe began and if so, I will exist as a spiritual being after its dissolution. I may have, in fact, been a part of the force that created the universe, assuming it did not occur by accident."

Often accompanying both spiritual and secular worldviews were questions regarding the capacity of earth-bound beings to fully comprehend the significance of their existence. Quoting the Bible, a minister observed that in this life, "we see through a dark glass. Only in the afterlife will we fully comprehend the mysteries of life. Recognizing our limitations may be among the purposes of our being here. Whether in this lifetime or whatever is next, awareness of the possibilities propels us forever forward."

Whatever our present views of our existence, our past experiences are powerful influences that continue to shape our lives. From a psychoanalytic perspective, our very early childhood experiences are particularly important. Many of our adult conflicts and anxieties have their origin in early childhood experiences buried but still active in the subconscious mind. Once these repressed experiences are

retrieved and resolved, our lives can become enriched and empowered with new insight and growth possibilities.

Like early childhood experiences stored in the subconscious,
our past-life experiences are forever with us. As already noted, we
are the totality of all our past experiences—they cannot be erased.
Furthermore, they are all relevant, and like forgotten childhood experiences, they can be retrieved and if needed, resolved. They invite
our attention and await our probes.

Our most recent past lifetimes often seem to command our special attention, beckoning us to explore them and uncover their relevance. For instance, parental rejection in a recent past lifetime can
result in an exaggerated need for acceptance in our present lifetime.
Along a different line, poverty and deprivation in a past lifetime
can result in a heightened drive for financial success and security in
the next.

Any unresolved traumatic experience in a past lifetime can energize an intense reaction in the next. For example, falling to one's
death in a past lifetime can be the source of a persistent fear of
heights in the next. Similarly, long-term imprisonment in a germ-
infested dungeon in a past lifetime can be a source of obsessive
cleanliness and compulsive hand-washing in the next.

An important part of our development is to figure out how to
overcome past-life adversities and transform them into new growth
resources. As earlier noted, past-life knowledge is therapeutic. Our
studies repeatedly found that past-life insight into the sources of
present-life dilemmas is almost always sufficient to resolve them.
The power of that insight is especially evident for such conditions
as obsessions, compulsions, and phobias which almost invariably
vanish in the light of past-life knowledge.

A particularly intense past-life experience can become a powerful force that expresses itself in a more generalized form in a subse-
quent lifetime. For instance, if you were betrayed by a lover in a
past lifetime, you may find yourself more cautious about entering

romantic relationships in your present lifetime. On the other hand, you may be more objective in your present love relationships, knowing that they are not always lasting. Along a similar line, a failed past-life friendship can result in greater selectivity in forming present friendships, or by extension, it can foster a general distrust of people in your present lifetime.

Fortunately, the achievements of our past lifetimes are always with us as important growth resources. They become a part of our "soul span," or the capacity of the evolving soul to stretch and grow across many lifetimes. For instance, if you successfully overcame adversity in a recent lifetime, you are probably better equipped to accommodate adversity in your present lifetime. Along a different line, if you achieved important humanitarian goals in a recent past lifetime, your humanitarian interests may remain very strong in the present, thanks to the strong reinforcement effect of recent past-life commitments.

On a very broad scale, knowledge of our past-life experiences, whether recent or distant, can equip us with the power we need to meet totally new life challenges. We become more empowered to overcome barriers, resolve conflicts, cope with stress, and build better social relationships, to list but a few of the possibilities.

All too often, however, we are enclosed, out of touch with ourselves and alienated from our past. We experience life passively or second-handedly through the interpretations and directions of others. Too often, we rely on others to do for us what we could more effectively do for ourselves. To expand our awareness and foster our personal growth, we must abandon the screens that filter knowledge and inhibit our growth. Only then can we focus with purpose on what is relevant to our existence.

In the chapters that follow, we will first examine our basic makeup as human beings—mentally, physically, and spiritually—with emphasis on the supremacy of the spirit over the mind and body. We will explore the existence of the soul as the indestructible but ever-changing essence of our being.

We will then explore self-hypnosis as a regression strategy, and review its effectiveness in providing past-life information related to our present existence. We will present a totally new hypnotic induction strategy for use in conjunction with a laboratory tested past-life regression procedure. We will examine the capacity of these procedures to provide a panoramic view of your personal past-life history. We will explore specifically the three major dimensions of your past life: your past lifetimes, your preexistence, and your life between lifetimes.

We will then explore a variety of discarnate manifestations, to include interactions with the departed, as important sources of insight concerning the afterlife and the nature of the discarnate realm. We will examine several accounts of ghosts and hauntings that seem to manifest the spirit world. We will explore several interdimensional strategies, to include table tipping and Interfacing, which can be used to initiate interactions with the other side.

Finally, we will explore out-of-body travel as a potential source of afterlife knowledge. We will present totally new out-of-body strategies specifically designed to explore the non-physical world.

Throughout the chapters that follow, our constant focus is on the dynamic repository of knowledge and potential existing within each of us and our capacity to experience it firsthand. Aside from that, we will explore the existence of spiritual specialists, including ministering guides, guardians, and master teachers—all of them poised to facilitate your quest for enlightenment and self-empowerment.

As you begin this important pilgrimage, here are a few practical guidelines and safeguards that will help you stay the course and empower you to reach new levels of personal growth and knowledge.

1. *Clarify your goals.* Your goal may be to explore in depth a particular past lifetime or to experience a panoramic view of your past life, from your preexistence forward. Your goal may be to explore only those past-life experiences that relate to your current life situation, such as a personal relationship, problem situation, or important decision. Whatever your goals, grab a piece of paper and write them down.

2. *Keep your probes focused.* Target in on what seems relevant at the moment.

3. *Keep your perspective and stay balanced.* Should your probes seem to get off course, back away and bring them to a comfortable level.

4. *Build your self-confidence.* Should you have uneasy moments during your past-life probes, remind yourself that you are in control. Your written goals will give direction to your probes and help bolster your resolve to achieve them.

5. *Invoke the guidance of your higher guides and teachers.* Get to know these spiritual growth specialists. They will accompany you and provide the support you need to achieve your goals.

6. *Fine-tune your past-life probes.* Periodically review your goals and evaluate the results of your probes. Look at your overall progress, and figure out where to go from there. Don't hesitate to make adjustments as needed.

7. *Keep a journal of your progress.* Record your regression experiences. Detailed documentation can identify significant events as well as small fragments of information that can be critical to your progress.

8. *Analyze your past-life findings.* Group them into categories and prioritize them. Look for relationships and central themes. Explore the present relevance of your findings.

9. *Use your past-life knowledge for decision making and problem solving.* Past-life knowledge can increase the quality and satisfaction of your life.

10. *Stay receptive to Cosmic Love.* The soul thrives on real love in whatever state or dimension it exists. Authentic Cosmic Love is the highest condition of freedom and growth. It can loose Karmic bands and energize your evolvement with amazing new growth possibilities.

## *Summary*

Your existence at this moment is a manifestation of your immortality as a conscious spirit being. As a soul, you are from everlasting to everlasting. Your past is forever within you and your future is forever before you. By embracing both, you enrich the moment.

Your evolution, like your existence, is forever. The greater your understanding of your existence in the fullness of its content and scope, the more effective you are in accelerating your own evolution while promoting the evolution of others. That's the challenge of each lifetime and each moment within it.

*Explore thyself. Herein are demanded the eye and the nerve.*
—Henry David Thoreau, Conclusions, Walden (1854)

# 2

# THE MIND-BODY-SPIRIT CONNECTION

We are at once a combination of mind, body, and spirit. There exists within these three interactive parts, however, a logical chain of command in which the body is subservient to the mind, and both the mind and body are subservient to the spirit. We've probably all experienced at one time or another those spiritually enlightening moments which reminded us of the preeminence of the spirit over the mind and body. Among the many examples are the potentially empowering sights and sounds of our natural surroundings—a magnificent sunset, a moonlit landscape, a powerful waterfall, an ocean view, a summer rainstorm, a waterfowl in flight, the starry heavens—each can balance and attune us in an instant to the wondrous power of the universe.

Because the mind, body, and spirit are interactive by nature, separating their functions into discrete categories is a very difficult needle to thread. Until now, the conventional scientific approach to resolve this dilemma has been simply to reduce the equation to mental and physical components only. According to this approach, mental and physical behavior can be either observed or inferred, therefore measured, quantified, and scientifically studied. The spiritual component, on the other hand, was seen for the most part as too slippery and illusory, thus not conducive to conventional scientific investigation. When considered at all, spiritual variables were usually subsumed under the category of either mental or physical.

At long last, conventional science has edged closer to recognizing the totality of the mind, body, and spirit interaction and the importance of each component and how it interacts with the others. We now know that to isolate or omit any one of these three variables would artificially modify the equation and limit our interpretation of the interaction. Furthermore, it would preclude any effort to promote mental, physical, and spiritual balance which is so essential to our total growth and self-fulfillment.

This book, while recognizing the contributions of other perspectives, focuses on that often neglected component—the spiritual, with emphasis on the role of the spirit as the critical factor in the mind-body-spirit interaction. At an individual level, it is the human spirit that energizes the mind and body. At a collective and more idealistic level, each soul being, while retaining its unique identity, unites with all others in absolute love to become the perfect supreme force, or as Ralph Waldo Emerson put it, the "over-soul" which animates the universe and embraces the earth in its bosom.

From a spiritual perspective, all our experiences of each lifetime—past, present, and future—must be eventually integrated into our soul being to facilitate our spiritual evolution. It is through that integrative process that we learn spiritual lessons which could be difficult if not impossible to learn in a discarnate state. That's the major reason why we are here—to learn and grow spiritually, while at the same time contributing to the spiritual evolution of others.

When we link human consciousness and experience exclusively to the brain, they become the sole property of the physical body. Awareness, perception, reasoning, memory, problem solving, attitudes, emotions, beliefs, and other mental functions become physically based and thus dependent on the survival (and well-being) of the physical body. Such a limited perspective fails to recognize that our present life experiences are always woven into the fabric of our non-biological or spiritual being where they join all the experiences of our past life as enduring growth resources. Together, they become endless components in our on-going spiritual unfoldment.

We know that mental and physical functions fail, and the body eventually wears out. Only the spiritual is forever. Given the permanence of the spirit and the temporal nature of the body, it follows that our spiritual evolution could require more than one lifetime, with each lifetime offering a new physical body and a dynamic re-embodiment of the spirit to result in totally new growth possibilities.

But how can we explain the temporal nature of the physical versus the permanent nature of the spiritual? As already noted, only that which has no beginning can be endless. All things physical, including the biological body, have a beginning and therefore an ending; all things spiritual, including the soul, have no beginning and therefore no ending.

But the permanence of the spirit can be more fully explained from a perspective which recognizes the basic biological and spiritual frameworks within which we all exist. We know that, by nature, we each have a genetic makeup called the genotype which provides the unique biological framework for our growth and development. It is temporal and therefore flawed. It ends with the physical body at death. Each new lifetime, consequently, requires a new body with a new genotype as the physical framework for growth and development in that lifetime.

Paralleling our physical genotype is a spiritual genotype which provides the spiritual framework for our growth and development. While the physical genotype ensures our uniqueness as a temporal biological being, the spiritual genotype ensures our uniqueness as a non-temporal spiritual being. Because it is non-physical, our spiritual genotype is forever—it is without either beginning or end. It is both spiritual and without flaw. It remains unbroken and unchanged from lifetime to lifetime. It therefore ensures our perpetual survival as a unique spiritual being. Simply put, the spiritual genotype is the perpetual framework within which the soul evolves.

From this perspective, the soul can be defined as that unique, immortal life-force essence without which we would not exist. The soul is not something I possess; it is that which I am forever. Rather than a physical body with a soul, I am a soul with a physical body. Each lifetime offers new opportunities to interact as a soul with a new biological counterpart and a new environment to maximize whatever growth potentials are afforded in that lifetime.

It is important to again emphasize that because the soul's basic framework is spiritual rather than physical, each soul by nature is perfect and indestructible. Souls evolve, but they cannot be damaged or broken. You are a soul being of perfection within an eternal reality. You existed as a soul before your first lifetime and you will exist as a soul beyond your last. In each lifetime, you existed as a soul in an embodied form that energized your physical body. You existed as a soul between lifetimes in disembodied form, thus providing a continuation of consciousness independent of physiology. The soul is, however, more than a state of consciousness—it is a state of spiritual being characterized by free will and self-determination.

Although identical biological genotypes are known to occur in instances of identical multiple births, there is absolutely no evidence suggesting the existence of identical spiritual genotypes. Among the billions of souls, each is unique, markedly different from all others. As souls, we have no carbon copies. Although you may have a close "soul mate" with whom you experience a special affinity, similarity, or connection, soul mates are distinctively independent entities, each with uniquely different spiritual genotypes.

While dramatic advances in biological cloning have been seen in recent years, there exists at present no shred of evidence suggesting even the remotest possibility of spiritual cloning. Furthermore, while mutations are common in biological evolution, there exists absolutely no evidence suggesting any instance of mutation in the evolution of souls.

The possibilities for differences in both biological and spiritual genotypes among individuals are endless. But unlike your biological makeup which changes from lifetime to lifetime, it must again be emphasized that the basic spiritual design of each soul exists forever in unaltered form. It is from everlasting to everlasting. Whether before your first incarnation or beyond your last, your identifying spiritual genotype as a soul is fixed. It is your permanent spiritual fingerprint, unlike that of any other soul. It provides the eternal framework within which you grow and develop as an immortal life-force entity.

From your existence before your first incarnation, which we call your preexistence, to the present and beyond, your potential as a living soul for growth, empowerment, and knowledge has no constricting boundaries. While the soul's genotype provides the framework for spiritual development, it prescribes absolutely no limits. Like your soul span, your growth span as a soul is from everlasting to everlasting, time without end.

Our existence as souls is trans-universal. In the embodied state, the soul is united with a physical body in a temporal space or physical reality which includes the planet earth and the physical universe as we know it. It's possible that your evolution as a soul included embodiment in another part of the universe, or for that matter, in another universe—possibly one that no longer exists. As we know, all things physical will eventually end; even the known universe which some scientists believe is already in the process of extinction.

While even universes may come and go, the soul is forever—it does not depend on the existence of physical reality. In the disembodied state, the soul exists in a spiritual environment or soul space which has no limits. Because the principles of linear time no longer apply, our existence in that space is both timeless and endless. Although some souls may have lived many lifetimes on earth whereas others may not have lived on earth at all, there are no age differences in soul space—souls are neither young nor old. They are instead forever ageless.

Implied in the word "soul" are suggestions of vitality, life, and of course, spirit. The soul is the very essence of your existence as a conscious, self-transcendent spiritual entity—alive, unique, and imperishable. Without the soul, you would not exist at all, but as a soul, you are alive forever. As a living soul (there is, in fact, no dead soul) your existence does not depend on this temporal, physical reality. Because you are spiritual, your exit from this life at death is but a transition, a crossing over to an even higher state of being. Simply put, the soul manifests the preexistent, immortal nature of your existence as a conscious spirit being.

Our existence as souls encompasses a totality that is difficult to imagine or comprehend. As earlier noted, our life span as spiritual entities is from everlasting to everlasting. Looking backward, I am from everlasting: looking forward, I am to everlasting. Since I am everlasting in both directions, the familiar, sometimes comforting limits of linear time, space, and all things physical simply do not apply. I am without either point of beginning or point of ending. What then is the destiny of souls? It is transcendent endlessness independent of time, space, or any other constricting reality.

Perhaps somewhat surprising, there are several Biblical references suggesting the preexistence of the soul as a conscious spirit entity. A notable example is God's message to Jeremiah: "Before I formed you in the womb I knew you, and before you were born I consecrated you . . ." (Jeremiah 2:5). Another excerpt speaks of the sons of God being present when the earth was formed: "On what were its bases sunk, or who laid its cornerstone, when the morning stars sang together, and all the sons of God shouted for joy?" (Job 38:6–7). The apostle Paul speaks of God as "he who had set me apart before I was born." (Gal. 1:15). Yet another passage refers to a preexistent state as follows: ". . . even as he (God) chose us in him before the foundation of the world." (Eph. 1:4). We find in 2 Enoch 23:5 this interesting observation: "All souls are prepared for eternity, before the composition of the earth." Chapter 32 also hints of Adam's preexistence. You will note that in these references the soul is referred to as the person (I, me, and us) rather than something possessed by the person.

Aside from the Biblical references suggesting preexistence, several early Christian writers were well-known proponents of the doctrine of the preexistence of souls. Origen, for instance, noted that the eternal goodness of God required that he disperse gifts to his creatures, and that there always existed rational creatures for this well-doing. Origen's concept further affirmed a preexistence in which immortal souls were able to make choices.[1]

Jewish sources also speak of preexistence as seen in the following prayer of Solomon: "As a child I was by nature well endowed, and a good soul fell to be my lot, or rather, being good, I entered an undefiled body." (Apocrapha, Wisdom of Solomon 8:19–20). He seems to be saying that his existence did not depend on embodiment; and that he, as a preexistent soul, entered an undefiled body. According to Jewish law, human "life" begins at birth; however the human soul is believed to exist before birth.

Traditional Judaism also believes that human existence continues after death, a view that allows for reincarnation through many

---

1. Bromiley, Geoffrey W. *Historical Theology*. Grand Rapids, MI: William B, Eerdmans Publishing Company, 1978, pp. 42–49.

lifetimes, according to some Orthodox Jews. In support of life after death, the Torah speaks of several noteworthy persons as having been "gathered to their people." Examples are Abraham, Ishmael, Isaac, Jacob, Moses, and Aaron.

Among the interesting Jewish views of the afterlife is the belief that the world is a "lobby" in which we prepare ourselves through study and good deeds to enter the "banquet hall." The emphasis in this metaphor, however, is on how to live life in the lobby rather than how to get into the banquet hall of heaven. We work and study out of a sense of love and duty, not in order to be rewarded or to get something in return.

Belief in reincarnation as a recurring manifestation of both pre-existence and immortality is commonly held by many mystically inclined Jews.[2] One school of thought holds that the resurrection is not a one-time event but rather an ongoing process in which souls are reborn either to continue improving the world or to complete some unfinished business. For each lifetime, the goals are essentially the same: Performing good deeds and using knowledge for the greatest good. How could anyone argue with that?

Many ancient civilizations, including the Greeks, Romans, and Egyptians, embraced the theory of reincarnation.[3] Also, the teachings of Hinduism and Buddhism include reincarnation as a reoccurring developmental phenomenon until the spirit reaches Nirvana, the final stage of human evolvement in which the individual soul is released from the wheel of life to become a part of God.

Several reincarnation concepts of Buddhist origin were later adopted into Theosophy, a popular mystical movement established

2. Freedman, David Noel. *The Anchor Bible Dictionary, Vol. 6,* New York: Doubleday, 1992, p. 161.

3. Durant, Will. *The Life of Greece.* New York: Simon and Schuster, 1939, pp. 134–138.

in New York in 1875.[4] According to this approach, reincarnation is a process of natural evolution ruled by divine justice called *Karma*. It is through reincarnation that the soul advances toward God.

Edgar Cayce, "the sleeping prophet," incorporated several Theosophical and Hindu concepts into his theory of reincarnation which also included orthodox Christian beliefs.[5] As souls, we incarnate on the earth plane to gain knowledge and experience. It is the creation and release of Karma, however, that perpetuates re-embodiment. For Cayce, Karma is simply an action in one lifetime that creates a cosmic effect in the next incarnation. These cosmic effects can result in joy or sadness, success or failure, and by enlargement, global advancement or decline, to mention but a few of the possibilities. Souls progress at their own rates to release themselves from the cycle of embodiment which is also called "the wheel of incarnation." In that process, the determining force is the soul's free will. Through wisdom gained during and between lifetimes comes understanding, and with understanding and positive action, release and transcendence to higher realms.

A popular view of reincarnation is based on the premise that life-force energy, while it may undergo transformation and change, is never lost. According to this view, consciousness and personal identity exist in life-force structural form, and as such, are never lost. Such survival phenomena as apparitions and hauntings along with deeply personal communications with the departed could thus be explained as the perseverance of life-force energy in meaningful discarnate form. According to this perspective, survival manifestations are consistently purposeful and empowerment driven.

---

4. Wilson, Colin. *The Occult: A History.* New York: Random House, 1971, pp. 330–349.

5. Puryear, Herbert B. *The Edgar Cayce Primer.* New York: Bantam Books, 1982, pp. 18–27.

They offer assurance of life after death and the continuation of personal consciousness and identity as well.

Finding your own way through the maze of views concerning preexistence, reincarnation, and the afterlife can be difficult and at times confusing. For me personally, the search for understanding started early in life with several childhood experiences suggesting past lifetimes.

One of my earliest experiences revolved around two apparently unrelated factors: a fear of water and an unexplained interest in France. It started during a third-grade classroom discussion of European geography when a series of colorful images began forming spontaneously in my mind. Though I had never been to Europe, I somehow knew the images to be French-related. As they continued to unfold like a movie, the images became increasingly specific: a port with several small boats docked along the abandoned shoreline; a row of familiar stone houses in the background, some of them three stories tall with balconies; and a small child playing at the shoreline and tossing stones into the water. Throughout the day, the images lingered in my mind.

That night in a dream, I became the child I had seen that day playing along the abandoned shoreline. While tossing stones into the water, I noticed at a distance a green bottle bobbing up and down. Though I could not swim, I waded cautiously into the water to retrieve the bottle, only to find myself being drawn uncontrollably into the dangerous deep.

I at once awakened, startled by the dream that so closely paralleled my classroom experience. Although I had never heard of past-life regression, I knew that the experiences had somehow tapped into a past lifetime in France, which would explain my very early interest in that country. Even more important, I wondered in the night whether my present fear of water could somehow be related to my death by drowning in that lifetime.

A few days later, I went swimming with my brothers for the first time. I knew before jumping right in that my fear of water had totally vanished. Fear had been replaced with freedom and sheer delight. Although a second childhood phobia, that of enclosed places, was yet to be resolved, I had discovered firsthand at a very early age the liberating power of past-life enlightenment. Little did I know at the time that I would devote much of my adult life as a psychologist to the study of reincarnation and the therapeutic power of past-life knowledge.

As an aside, a noted British psychic who was conducting a seminar a few years ago at Athens State University offered interesting confirmation of my early childhood regression experience. Although she had been given no information concerning the experience, she described in detail my past lifetime in the little French port of Bonyuls-sur-mer on the Mediterranean. She added that my lifetime in France had been cut short by drowning.

Several other childhood experiences were to spur an even greater interest in reincarnation. Among the most vivid were the rainmaking rituals conducted by a local Native American during summer droughts which were common in the Deep South where I grew up. During these "dry spells," as they were called, area farmers including my father occasionally gathered for the ritual led by the so-called "rainmaker" who was himself a farmer.

I can only guess at how old the tall, muscular built man with hawk-like features was, probably no more than fifty. For the outdoor ritual, he would stand like a statue on a knoll near his house, surrounded by flat, brown terrain. With local residents forming an outer circle, he would turn his cupped palms upward, and after articulating a short series of strong but unintelligible sounds, he would slowly bring his hands together, hold them for a moment, and then fling them upward with the speed and grace of a dove taking flight as if to send into space whatever he had gathered in his hands. His face more pale than before, he would then conclude the ritual in a soft voice, not the strong tomes we had heard earlier, with the simple statement: "We will now let it rain."

Within a few hours, the clouds would gather and the rains would come in welcomed abundance. According to area farmers, the rainmaker's rituals never failed to produce the much-needed rain.

Interestingly, during the so-called "wet spells" when the rains came in over abundance for many days, the dark-haired rainmaker consistently refused to end the rain, saying that it would "go against nature to unmake rain." To make rain, he claimed in his metallic voice, was to work in harmony with nature, not against it.

Having witnessed the rainmaker's amazing ability to bring forth rain, I along with several neighboring children decided to test his ability to produce a winter snowfall. Although snow was rare for our region, he consented with the approval of our parents to make snow. With the group of children assembled on a late winter afternoon, he performed on the same knoll an outdoor ritual similar to rainmaking but with noticeably different sounds and a pace that was considerably slower. He concluded the brief ritual with the words: "We will now let it snow."

That night, a northern front moved in, and like a fairy tale come true, it began to snow. The snow continued throughout the night and well into the following day, blanketing the earth with around four inches which was considered a major snowfall for the region. Never again, however, would the rainmaker consent to produce snow. "Making it snow," he insisted, "would be unmindful of the animals."

Whenever asked to explain his extraordinary skills, the rainmaker would only reply, "They are from another time and place." Years later when I last saw him, I asked privately whether his rainmaking powers were from a past lifetime. His face by then set in lines that seemed too old for his age, he smiled knowingly but replied exactly as before, "They are from another time and place."

Among my other early memories are the many remarkable feats of my grandmother whose skills also included the incredible ability to influence weather conditions. Having acquired these skills "from back in time," she was not reluctant to use them whenever the situation "called for them," as she put it.

Growing up in a sparsely settled area of the Deep South, I often visited my grandparents who lived within bicycling range. On one particular visit, I watched my grandmother break apart an approaching wall cloud, the type known to spawn tornadoes. I looked on in amazement from a window as this energetic woman—elegantly dressed in black as usual—hurried from the house, grabbed an axe, brought it overhead, and forcefully struck it into the ground, all within a few seconds. Then standing tall and slender before the ax, which was fixed firmly at an angle in the ground, she reached boldly toward the dark cloud with her hands turned outward as if to repel it. Almost instantly, the cloud became more turbulent before splitting vertically into two jagged sections and then scattering into small parts to let the sun burst through! The silhouette of my grandmother standing steadfastly before an ax anchored in the ground, with her arms extended toward an ominous cloud, remains to this day indelibly etched in my mind.

In a later equally unforgettable incident, I witnessed—or perhaps better put, experienced—what may have been my grandmother's ability to defy gravity. Following her visit on a rainy Friday afternoon, my two brothers and I accompanied her in her horse-drawn surrey back to her house for the weekend, as we often did. Although my grandparents owned an automobile, my grandmother preferred the surrey for local travel, partly because it had belonged to her mother who had come to America from Germany in the late 1800s. But she seemed not so much attached to the surrey as to the magnificently regal black horse named Tess that drew it.

With my grandmother seated up front at the reins and the three of us settled in the back seat, we embarked on the two-mile journey.

Already it was nearing dark, and the cold winter rain, now falling heavily, made travel on the unpaved country road difficult.

Finally, with the lights of her tall colonial house set among great oaks coming into view on a distant hill, we approached a very wide stream swollen well beyond its banks, its bridge totally submerged. Upon stopping the surrey near the edge of the turbulent stream, my grandmother dressed in a black cape and hat turned to us, her face more pale than normal against the darkness. She instructed us to lie on the surrey's floor and to cover ourselves from head to foot with the heavy lap robe stored under the seat. After checking to see that our heads were covered, she calmly added, "Now close your eyes, and do not move."

Under cover of the robe, we felt the surrey moving gently upward and then smoothly forward in absolute silence, as if gliding on thin air. Soon, the horse drawn surrey came to rest with an easy bounce on the other side of the rushing stream. Once we were back in our seats as before, my youngest brother blurted out, "That was better than a Ferris wheel ride at the county fair!"

When we finally arrived, my grandfather, tall and distinguished, met us at the door and escorted us into the parlor where we waited before a roaring fireplace while he attended to Tess. Although stable hands were available, my grandfather always took care of Tess personally. More than once I heard him refer to Tess as Priestess, which I assumed was her formal name.

Later on, as we all gathered in the dining room for a candlelit dinner, the conversation turned to the events of the day, but without mention of the swollen stream and our incredible flight over it. Yet throughout dinner I could think of nothing else. Images of Moses parting the Red Sea and Jesus walking upon the water flashed into my mind, but they paled in comparison to a horse-drawn carriage being borne aloft, gliding gently over a wide, turbulent stream.

As the night wore on, we gathered once again before the roaring fireplace in the parlor where finally, the conversation turned to the stormy weather outside. I had been waiting for that moment! I quickly brought up the swollen stream with its submerged bridge and summoned the boldness to ask my grandmother how we had so easily crossed it. With my grandfather at her side, she answered without hesitation, "Some things we learn in this life; some things we learn after this life; and some things we learn before this life. It really doesn't matter when or where we learn them, it's how we use them that counts." My grandfather nodded in agreement. We then turned our attention to popping popcorn on the open fire.

In bed that night, with the lights out and the house quiet, I reflected on the day's events and wondered what had really transpired at the swollen stream. Had my grandmother acquired that amazing power in a past life, or was it something she had learned in her present lifetime? Could there be something magical about the carriage or the lap robe—I had heard of a magic carpet but never a magic lap robe! And then there was something about Tess. Was that amazing horse my Grandmother's accomplice in that incredible feat? My grandparents had often reminded us that animals are spirit beings of dignity and worth. Whenever you looked close up into Tess's eyes, you sensed a great depth of spirituality. If her formal name were indeed Priestess, could Tess be a reincarnated high priestess with magical powers of her own? "Why not?" I thought. I fell asleep imagining that I would perhaps one day discover the secrets of such incredible power.

Many years later while teaching a college course in parapsychology, I was reminded of my grandmother's flight by carriage over the swollen stream. During a discussion of psychokinesis (PK), a military student who had served in Vietnam recalled having seen Vietnamese children at play dashing out upon the deep inland waterways and literally running on the surface of the water to retrieve

a ball or other floating object. He added, "I know that seems unbe-
lievable to most people," to which I responded, "To me, it's not un-
believable at all!"

My grandparents remained active and in near excellent health
until their transition in their nineties—they died within two weeks
of each other. It was within a few days of their crossing that Tess
also crossed over to join them. My grandparents firmly believed in
the afterlife existence of animals as spirit beings. I remember having seen my grandfather time and again gently comfort dying animals as if to assist them in their transition to the other side. He believed that the best measure of how far a culture had advanced
rested in the nature of its treatment of animals.

Soon after my grandparents and Tess crossed over, the lap
robe—its edges by then showing considerable wear—was found in
a chest carefully folded with a note and my name on it. Made of
homespun wool, the beautiful robe with its black underside and
top design of two large red roses remains in my keeping as a cher-
ished reminder of their magical lives together (see figure 1).

These and many other early experiences in my small, easy world
as a young child richly colored my view of life and laid the ground-
work for my enduring interest in psychic phenomena, reincarnation, and the empowerment possibilities of past-life enlightenment.
They suggested many wondrous opportunities beyond my known
world as well as a vast, inner reservoir of potential just waiting to be
probed. I became convinced early in life that there are absolutely no
limits to the possibilities when you tap into the powers within. In
the chapters that follow, we will explore the strategies needed to do
just that.

*Figure 1. The Lap Robe.*

## *Summary*

Souls evolve. Birth and death are life transitions within the endless evolution of souls. Both are passages that signal a new beginning with new growth possibilities. Both disengage the past to empower our embarkment on a new life journey in a new dimension. Each new lifetime offers new growth opportunities in the physical world; each new after lifetime offers new growth opportunities in the spirit world.

All the empowering resources of our past remain forever with us. At birth, we bring our past with us into a new lifetime; at death we take our past with us into the afterlife. Because they are integrated into the soul, the accomplishments of each lifetime are forever with us.

To assume that death of the physical body erases the accomplishments of a lifetime is both irrational and inaccurate. Such an assumption contradicts the very nature of the soul as a dynamic, indestructible life force that is forever evolving.

*Be thine own palace, or the world's thy jail.*
—John Dunne, "To Sir Henry Wotton" (1633)

# SELF-HYPNOSIS AND
# PAST-LIFE REGRESSION

Possibly no other part of our being is more critical to our personal growth and development than that vast inner region known as the subconscious. Rich in knowledge and underdeveloped potentials, it challenges us to probe its depths and activate its dormant powers.

No one but you can ever have full access to your personal subconscious. It's your private world—a vast repository of all your personal experiences not presently available to conscious awareness. Through your dreams, intuitive impressions, psychic insights, and a host of other channels, it invites your interaction with the simple, persistent message: I exist.

Although it exists beyond the range of normal conscious awareness, the subconscious is interwoven into the very fabric of our being as a critical component of our soul consciousness. It is central to our existence, not as an accumulation of extraneous baggage, but rather as a gold mine of knowledge and growth possibilities.

Strange as it may seem at first glance, the wisdom of the subconscious often surpasses that of conscious awareness. For each of us, every unknown experience, from our preexistence to the present, is stored in the subconscious, just waiting to be tapped into. Beyond that vast content, the subconscious is a valuable storehouse of insight and growth potential. It is an advanced teacher, guide, counselor, and growth facilitator. In its wisdom, it knows that new growth is best when it demands our highest efforts, and that new knowledge is more meaningful when it challenges our active participation. By probing its depths, you will discover for yourself the wonder and power of self-discovery.

For many years, hypnosis requiring the assistance of a trained hypnotist has been one of the most popular strategies for probing the subconscious and unleashing its potentials. Using that approach, discovering past-life experiences stored beyond conscious awareness is under the direction or guidance of a consulting hypnotist who is often called a past-life hypnotherapist. All that's required are a receptive subject, a trained hypnotist, and in most instances, a considerable fee for services rendered.

In our surveys, a majority of respondents who had sought assistance in uncovering their past lives did turn in fact to consulting hypnotists (TR 31). For the most part, the hypnotists were psychologists, counselors, or other professionals with specialized training in hypnosis. Occasionally, they were trance psychics who themselves entered a self-induced trance state during which they gave past-life readings to their clients. In most instances, however, the hypnotists induced a trance state in their subjects who were then regressed to their past lives.

Somewhat to our surprise, our surveys found that a large majority of subjects who had turned to consulting hypnotists for past-life regression were dissatisfied with the results. Over three-fourths of them reported either failure to enter a sufficient trance state to begin with, or else failure to experience satisfactory past-life regression once under hypnosis. They emerged from their hypnosis sessions with serious doubts about the value of their regression experiences.

For subjects of our surveys who turned to psychic consultants for either hypnosis or past-life readings, the dissatisfaction with the experience was even greater. They often questioned the psychic's qualifications and claims of success. Subjects who had been regressed by psychics or who had received past-life readings from multiple psychics were particularly skeptical because of wide discrepancies and frequent contradictions found in the results.

Equally as unsettling as these findings, our interviews with hypnotists—including psychologists, counselors, and psychics—found that their personal beliefs almost invariably influenced the results of their sessions (TR 33). Although their beliefs varied greatly, they tended to orchestrate their sessions, often through subtle suggestions, so that their beliefs were communicated to their hypnotized subjects. This finding was especially evident in sessions involving the spirit realm. For instance, consulting hypnotists who viewed the afterlife as a highly structured situation with discarnate classifications, forums, experts, councils, and fixed procedures invariably incorporated their own views into their regression sessions, thus strongly contaminating the outcomes. Our studies further found that hypnotists tended to give more attention to their subjects' discarnate experiences that were consistent with their own views, whereas contradictory experiences were largely ignored and in some instances, either contradicted or challenged by the hypnotist.

Similarly, consulting hypnotists often used rigid regression procedures that shaped the perceptions of their subjects and guided them into experiences consistent with their own frame of reference. One hypnotist, for instance, characteristically structured for his hypnotized subjects an after-lifetime situation in which a "higher council of patriarchs" always evaluated discarnates and assigned certain tasks for them to accomplish before they could be reincarnated. When I questioned him concerning this part of the regression session, he replied, "We all know that after each lifetime, we must appear before a higher council that evaluates our most recent past lifetime and assigns certain tasks accordingly. These must be completed before our next lifetime." Such orientations will obviously influence the outcomes of any regression effort.

The time is long past due for us to take a serious look at the 800-pound gorilla of past-life regression, not to discredit professional hypnotists and other credible past-life specialists, but rather to develop more effective approaches in probing past-life experiences. As I've said, your subconscious is your private world. Self-discovery and personal growth are the major goals of past-life regression. By discovering your past-life experiences for yourself, you can better decide for yourself on how best to use them. To be told about them by others or to be directed by others in your efforts to discover them is of minimal value at best. It would seem only reasonable that by shifting responsibility for regression away from the outside regression specialist to the individual subject of regression could greatly increase the relevance and rewards of past-life regression. Past-life enlightenment through self-discovery leads invariably to ways of using it for the greatest good.

## Self-hypnosis and Past-life Regression

Given the fact that your best personal hypnotist exists within yourself, it follows that the most effective hypnotic regression procedure would logically focus on that inner specialist. Two self-administered procedures were developed in our labs to activate that specialist. The first procedure, a self-hypnosis strategy known as **EM/RC**, incorporates eye movement (EM) and reverse counting (RC) into a procedure designed to induce a trance state conducive to past-life regression (TR 5). This procedure accepts the premise that within each of us is not only a master hypnotist but also a master teacher, therapist, healer, and psychic, all of which are receptive to our probes. Our task is to find ways of getting in touch with those powers. EM/RC was designed to meet that challenge.

The second procedure known as **Past-life Corridor** was developed as a self-regression strategy for use in concert with EM/RC (TR 3). The Past-life Corridor, as we will later see, contains doors representing each of your past lifetimes as well as your preexistence and life between lifetimes. Each door is a living gateway to your past. When used together, EM/RC and Past-life Corridor provide the essentials for successful hypnosis and regression to your past life in its totality.

It is important to point out here that in our development and use of these procedures, no effort was made at any time to influence the beliefs of our research subjects, nor to shape in any way their regression experiences. Your past experiences are unique to you, and you have sole ownership of them. In our labs, Topic A was to develop workable tools for self-discovery of those experiences. It was our position that, once given the tools, you could explore for yourself the past-life experiences that are presently relevant to you. Once given that knowledge, you can draw your own conclusions independent of the opinions and influences of others.

In our labs, EM/RC and Past-life Corridor when used together were found to be the most effective strategy known for retrieving relevant past-life experiences. Although they lack the bells and whistles of other approaches, these self-administered procedures typically extinguish any semblance of resistance, either to hypnosis or past-life regression. With the subject in command of the induction and regression process, the degree of satisfaction for this do-it-yourself approach was at a level far greater than that of any other known induction or regression strategy. The follow-on ratings by our subjects regarding the relevance of their regression experiences were likewise very high.

Specifically designed to induce a hypnotic state that facilitates past-life regression, the EM/RC procedure incorporates age-regression to an early childhood experience which then becomes the springboard for past-life regression using the Past-life Corridor. Later during the trance, the same childhood experience becomes the portal for re-entry into your present lifetime. It is important to keep in mind that you are the keeper of that portal, and you can return to it at any time during the regression experience.

Both EM/RC and the Past-life Corridor, like all the strategies presented in this book, are self-administered throughout. They are based on a simple three-fold premise: first, you know yourself better than anyone else; second, all your past experiences exist within yourself as an integral part of your being; and third, you are your own best hypnotist and past-life regression specialist. All the resources you need are within yourself and now accessible to you.

Together, EM/RC and the Past-life Corridor can put you in touch with that knowing, innermost part of yourself and safely guide your probes into your past. With practice, these procedures can empower you to discover whatever you need to know at the moment about your past. Beyond that, they can reveal the relevance of your past to your future. They provide an invaluable path to self-discovery with signposts to guide you all along the way.

Our past-life studies using these procedures suggested over and over again that there exists a higher—or dare I say it—divine intelligence that knows what exists behind each door (TR 8). That intelligence can illuminate a particular door in the Past-life Corridor and draw your attention to it. That intelligence knows that out of a given past lifetime of experience, a certain experience can hold critical relevance for you at this moment in your life. It can reveal that segment, or it can present a past lifetime in its full scope. But best of all, that higher intelligence is within yourself—it is a part of you. It can point the way for you to go, but it's up to you to embark on the journey. It can illuminate a past-life door, but it's up to you to open it. It can reveal which past-lifetime and which specific experience in that lifetime hold greatest relevance for you at this time in your life.

Guided by that higher intelligence within, you can experience through these procedures an overview of all your past lifetimes from which you can choose a particular lifetime to explore, either as a spectator or active participant. Once you've selected a particular lifetime, you can experience a small but relevant segment of it, or you can move backward or forward within that lifetime to experience it in its greater fullness. Upon return to the corridor after a particular past-lifetime experience, you can, should you decide to do so, open the between lifetime door at the corridor's end to discover relevant afterlife experiences for that particular lifetime. Later in this book, we will discuss the between lifetime as well as preexistence dimensions of your past life.

It is important to keep in mind that the Past-life Corridor with its many doors to an incredible wealth of experience is actually within yourself. With these procedures, you can open the doors of your choosing. You will discover that no aspect of your past is beyond your probe.

On a practical note, these procedures should be used only in a comfortable, safe, and quiet setting completely free of distractions. They should never be used under conditions requiring alertness and vigilance, such as while driving or operating machinery. It is important to read both procedures in their entirety before starting. You will find them easy to follow, but practice is usually required to maximize their effectiveness. Here are the two procedures which together require approximately one hour.

## *EM/RC and Past-life Corridor*

### Step 1. EM/RC Preliminaries

Begin the EM/RC procedure by settling back into a comfortable, reclining position with your legs uncrossed and your hands resting at your sides. As you become increasingly relaxed, take in several breaths, inhaling deeply and exhaling slowly. Develop a slow, rhythmic breathing pattern as you clear your mind of all active thought. Notice your sense of peace with yourself and the world.

At this early stage, give yourself permission to enter hypnosis and while in the trance state, to travel into your past to retrieve whatever is relevant for you at the moment. Affirm that you will be in full and complete control throughout the trance experience. Further affirm that you can at any moment exit hypnosis by simply counting upward from one to five.

### Step 2. Trance Induction

You are now ready to initiate the trance state using a combination of eye movement and reverse counting. Tell yourself that by shifting your eyes from side to side as you count backward from ten, you will enter the trance state. Further affirm that each count backward will take you deeper and deeper until you reach a successful trance state on the count of one.

As your eyes remain open, begin the procedure by slowly shifting your eyes upward and to your right without turning your head on the count of ten. Hold your eyes in that upper right position until they begin to tire. Then slowly shift your eyes downward and then upward to your left on the count of nine and hold them in that upper left position until they begin to tire. As you shift your eyes from side to side on each count, develop a rhythmic downward and then upward swinging movement, always holding your eyes in each upper position. You will notice your eyes becoming increasingly tired as you continue the rhythmic eye-movement and reverse-counting combination. Upon reaching the count of one, slowly close your eyes while still holding them in the upper position. Once your eyes are closed, let them return to their normal position. With your eyes now comfortably closed and the muscles around them relaxed, let yourself slowly enter the trance state.

## Step 3. Deepening the Trance

As your eyes remain closed, deepen the trance state by taking a few moments to envision a very peaceful scene and then letting yourself become progressively relaxed from your head downward. Notice first the relaxation around your eyes and then let it spread slowly over your face and then into your neck and shoulders. Let the relaxation then radiate into your shoulders and arms, right through the tips of your fingers. Then notice the relaxation in your chest and let it spread deep into your abdomen. Let the relaxation extend slowly downward, soaking into your hips, thighs, lower legs, and finally right through the tips of your toes.

As you remain comfortable and deeply relaxed, envision again a very peaceful scene—either the one you pictured earlier or a totally new one. Notice the pleasing details of the mental image, and let yourself absorb the tranquility of the scene. You are now at complete peace with yourself and the world.

You can at this point reach an even deeper level of hypnosis, should you decide to do so, by focusing your full attention on the little finger of either hand, noticing its weight, tingling, warmth, and so forth, and then mentally replacing these sensations with numbness. As your finger remains numb, let yourself go deeper and deeper into hypnosis. When you reach the desired trance level, allow the feeling to return and then move your finger slightly as a signal of your success. Again remind yourself that you are in full and complete control of the trance state.

(Note: With practice, you will find that the EM/RC procedure is a very flexible induction procedure that can be easily tailored to your own preferences and needs. Some subjects find that the rhythmic eye movement independent of reverse counting is sufficient to induce the trance state. Almost everyone will find that inserting such suggestions as "more and more relaxed" and "deeper and deeper" at times throughout the procedure facilitates the induction process. Should you enter a satisfactory trance state before completing the full EM/RC procedure, simply proceed to the next stage: regression to childhood.)

## Step 4. Regression to Childhood

Once you've reached a successful trance level, begin your regression to childhood by envisioning a pleasant childhood situation in which you participated in a festive occasion—perhaps a birthday party or holiday celebration. Take plenty of time to become a part of the childhood experience and give yourself permission to use it as a springboard for past-life regression. You are now ready to begin the past-life regression experience using the Past-life Corridor procedure.

## Step 5. Past-life Corridor Preliminaries

While remaining in the trance state, give yourself permission to use the trance as a vehicle for past-life regression. Re-affirm that you will experience only those past-life events that are relevant and presently useful to you. Remind yourself that you can at any moment end the trance state and return safely to the present by simply counting upward from one to five.

Affirm that you will be protected and secure throughout the regression experience. You may decide at this point to invite a personal spirit guide to accompany you in your past-life probes.

Tell yourself that upon later exiting hypnosis, you will recall those past-life experiences that are important to you at this time. Affirm your ability to use past-life insight productively to enrich your present life and promote your future growth. Remind yourself that you will remain in full control throughout the regression experience.

## Step 6. Entering the Past-life Corridor

You are now ready to enter the Past-life Corridor. Notice the brightly illuminated corridor stretching into the distance. Your personal past-life corridor is unique to you—it is unlike any other corridor. It can be of any combination of materials, colors, and shapes. It can, for instance, be of stone, marble, or gold. The colors can range from the boldest shades to the most delicate pastels.

On the sides of the corridor you will notice doors, one for each of your past lifetimes. If your present lifetime is your first, there will be no side doors. But if you have lived many lifetimes, there will, of course, be many doors. They, like the hallway itself, can be of a variety of materials, such as jade, amber, or glass. Their shapes can likewise vary, to include rectangular, round, heart-shaped, or oval, to list but a few of the possibilities.

Behind each door is a past lifetime, with the doors closest to the corridor's entrance representing your most recent lifetimes, and the doors in the distance representing your earlier lifetimes. By opening the door of your choosing, you can experience the events of that life which hold relevance for you at the moment.

At the far end of the bright corridor, you will notice a resplendent door representing your preexistence. Provided you have lived a previous lifetime, you will notice a second bright door situated to the right of the preexistence door. It represents your life between lifetimes in the spirit realm. Together, the two luminous side-by-side doors provide a gateway to the spirit realm as you experienced it in past life. You can at will open either door to gain the information you need concerning these important dimensions of your past. (In our studies, less than three percent of our subjects experienced no previous lifetimes upon entering the Past-life Corridor. For them, the corridor included only the preexistence door.)

### Step 7. Experiencing Past Lifetimes

Upon entering the corridor, select the door that holds particular appeal for you at the moment. Almost always, it is the door that first commanded your attention, or the door that stands out as brightest among the others. Upon approaching the door, you may decide to open the door and view from the doorway the past life it represents, or you can step through the door and become an active participant in that past life.

As you experience the past lifetime you selected, either from the open door as a spectator or from beyond the door as an active participant, you can at will shift your awareness either forward or backward to experience it in as much scope and detail as you prefer. To shift forward, count 1, 2, 3; to shift backward, count 3, 2, 1.

Once regression to a particular past lifetime is complete, you can leave that lifetime by simply returning to the corridor and closing the door behind you. At this point, you may wish to explore another past lifetime by opening another past-lifetime door. To promote recall of the regression experience, it is recommended that no more than two past lifetimes be experienced during a particular regression session.

(Note: We should note here that should you wish to explore the afterlife that followed a given past lifetime, you can open the life-between-lifetimes door at the end of the corridor. Opening that afterlife door immediately following your regression to a particular past lifetime ensures that the afterlife depicted is the immediate follow-on to that lifetime. The next chapter explores in detail life-between-lifetimes as well as preexistence and ways of experiencing these important realms of your past.)

### Step 8. Conclusion

To exit the Past-life Corridor, give yourself permission to return first to the childhood situation you experienced earlier, and from there, into the present. Upon your return to the present and before exiting the trance state, affirm that you will successfully recall the regression experience in as much detail as needed and that you will understand its full relevance.

To end the trance state, count slowly from one to five with interjected suggestions of alertness and well-being. On the count of five, open your eyes and take a few moments to reflect on the experience.

Many of our subjects found that upon opening a particular door, the past lifetime it represented unfolded before them like a movie. The more highly relevant experiences of that lifetime often appeared in bright detail, thereby commanding attention and inviting interaction.

Subjects who remain spectator observers during their regression often describe their experiences as three dimensional in which relevant aspects of their past were depicted in colorful detail. In these dramatizations, our regression subjects invariably recognized themselves, even when they were pictured as the other gender or another race.

In contrast to spectators, active participants who "stepped into" their past lifetime experienced it close up as though they were actually there interacting with their surroundings and others exactly as they did in that past lifetime. Both spectators and participants alike were typically aware of their past-life personal identity and life situation as well as the historical settings and geographical location of the past lifetime depicted.

The EM/RC procedure can be supplemented as needed with a variety of trance deepening techniques, or if you prefer, you can use a totally different induction approach, perhaps one you have already mastered. Although EM/RC is particularly conducive to past-life regression, some subjects prefer alternative strategies, including the popular hand levitation technique. In this procedure, the hand at rest on your thigh gently rises at your suggestion to touch your forehead, thereby inducing the trance state. A second popular procedure is eye fixation in which attention is centered on a fixed object to facilitate the upward gaze and thus promote the trance state. Both of these techniques use suggestions of drowsiness along with a variety of other deepening strategies.

Regardless of the strategies used, you will find that with practice, your ability to enter hypnosis and regress to designated past lifetimes will improve. Given sufficient practice and experience, you may successfully master, like many of our subjects, the highest form of trance induction known—the ability to enter hypnosis through sheer intent alone.

Although EM/RC was developed in our labs as a self-induction procedure specifically for use in combination with Past-life Corridor, it can be easily adapted for other uses, including such wide-ranging applications as losing weight, breaking unwanted habits, managing pain, improving memory, and even slowing aging.

As with EM/RC, you can revise the Past-life Corridor procedure to meet your personal preferences, or you can substitute a totally different regression strategy. Although Past-life Corridor has shown remarkable effectiveness with subjects of different backgrounds and experience, you may prefer an alternative procedure, such as the **Blank Screen Technique** which was also developed in our labs. This technique uses imagery of a blank screen upon which appears scenes related to your past lifetimes. Once a scene appears, you can either view the unfolding images or actually enter the action of the scene to experience past-life happenings firsthand and in great detail. From there, you can either "fast forward" by counting 1, 2, 3, or "fast-backward" by counting 3, 2, 1 to experience a particular past lifetime in greater scope and detail.

To maximize the effectiveness of your regression experiences, it is important to maintain a detailed journal of each session. Research your journal entries and take time to reflect upon them, keeping in mind that all experiences, past and present, are purposeful. You will eventually discover the relevance of your regression experiences to your present-life situation.

Whatever strategies you choose for inducing the trance state and experiencing your past life, don't rush it—take plenty of time to enjoy the regression experience and discover its relevance. It is important again to emphasize that the best specialist—whether for hypnosis or past-life regression—exists within yourself. After all, you know yourself better than anyone else, and all your past-life experiences remain a critical part of your growth history. By acquiring the skills to reconnect to them, you can discover for yourself all you need to know about your past and its relevance to you at this moment in your life.

## The Past-life Journal

Keeping a detailed past-life journal of each regression session is important for several reasons. First, it provides a review and thus promotes retention of the regression experience. Second, it promotes insight and discovery of the underlying relevance of the experience. Third, it provides a written past-life record which you can then research and possibly verify.

In keeping a past-life journal, provide with each entry sufficient space for reporting your follow-on impressions and research finding.

Here are the past-life journal entries of three subjects who used EM/RC and Past-life Corridor to explore their past lifetimes. The entries, as you will note, include a later follow-on entry.

**Subject l: Bank executive, female, age 32**
**Journal Entry:**
This was my first experience with the EM/RC induction method, and I was actually surprised at how receptive I was to it. Upon completing the side-to-side eye movements, I knew I was in the trance state. But just to be certain, I gave myself the finger anesthesia test. My little finger became so numb that I couldn't move it. I restored

the feeling and seemed to go even deeper into hypnosis, though I knew I was still in full control.

I then regressed to an early childhood experience in which I was helping my mother decorate a cake. I used pieces of candy to outline a snowman, and then filled the figure in with smaller pieces of candy. I then turned my attention backward in time to the Past-life Corridor.

I saw a very long corridor with many doors on each side. Over the corridor was a crystal clear glass ceiling that revealed a bright starry heaven. Looking down the corridor which was flooded with clear, soft light, I was astonished at the many doors of various colors, materials, and shapes. At first, a distant door near the end of the corridor commanded my attention. A crystalline door shimmering and radiating light in all directions, it stood out among all the others, but I was for some reason hesitant to enter it.

Suddenly, a door closer at hand drew my attention. As I looked at the door, a halo of bright rainbow colors began to form around it. Although surrounded by radiance, the door itself was of hand hewn wood with a rose delicately carved upon it. It evoked such curiosity that I felt compelled to open it.

As I touched the rustic door, it flung open to reveal a scene in which I was surrounded by a disorderly multitude of people, some of them laughing boisterously and others shouting obscenities. Although unsure of what was happening, I felt compelled to step through the door. Once inside, I was no longer an objective observer, but rather the target of the riotous crowd. I was bound and then beaten, cut and stabbed with knives, and stoned. After what seemed like hours of excruciating pain, I was thrown across a blood-soaked structure where I knew I was about to be beheaded. A jesting spectator bellowed out addressing me as Dorothea and derisively requesting that I send him roses and apples from paradise.

At that point, the unfolding events became so painful that I seemed to disengage my body. I retreated to the corridor and witnessed from the doorway my own execution.

Finally, I returned to my present lifetime, first as a child decorating a cake, and from there, into the present.

## Follow-on Entry:

Given the nature of the regression experience, I was surprised at the peaceful acceptance I felt upon opening my eyes. The experience was so profound that I knew that it had current relevance. I connected it immediately to certain facts: I have a daughter named Dorothea, the rose is my favorite flower, and I love apples—I even grow them. But beyond these, I was convinced that my experience had important practical relevance.

I already knew the name Dorothea was Greek for "gift of God," but I did not know that she was a Christian martyr who was tortured and decapitated in the bloody persecution of the Roman emperor, Diocletian, early in the third century A.D. My research led, however, to another interesting discovery: A jesting spectator, whose name was Theophilus, did indeed ask the dying Dorothea to send him roses and apples from paradise. Miraculously, his request was apparently fulfilled—he was soon to mysteriously receive a gift of roses and apples. Theophilus was converted by the miracle, only to suffer the same fate as Dorothea—he was later tortured and decapitated for his faith.

Before my regression experience, I had been fearful of large crowds throughout my life. Even as a young child, I was always uncomfortable around people, and as an adult, I avoided large public gatherings as much as possible, basically out of concern that something would go wrong. After my regression experience, I knew that my life-long fear of crowds was related to my public execution in a past-life. Armed with that new insight, I decided to attend several large public gatherings and found, to my relief, that I was comfortable, relaxed, and totally liberated from the fear of large crowds.

Was I Dorothea in a past lifetime, and was the fear of crowds a reaction to my public execution in that life? It really doesn't matter so much, because whether I was Dorothea or not, the past-life regression was one of the most empowering experiences of my life.

(Note: St. Dorothea's festival is celebrated on February 6 by the Roman Catholic Church.)

This subject's journal entry reflects the importance of follow-on research that often ferrets out the important relevance of the past-life experience. For this subject, it heightened both the enlightening and therapeutic effects of the experience.

In a later regression session, she decided to return to the door with the rose carving. The door was the same, but the experiences behind it were markedly different. She experienced, rather than her death, segments from a happy childhood in which she was taught the importance of honesty and consideration of others. As a bank executive, those values held for her a special relevance.

## Subject 2: Mechanical engineer, male, age 28
### Journal Entry:

I've always wondered whether I had actually lived past lives, but somehow I could not bring myself to be hypnotized, let alone regressed into my unknown past. To me, that was scary—like walking along a strange path with many pitfalls in total darkness! But when I learned of Dr. Slate's self-regression study, I volunteered to try it, since it seemed to have all the necessary built-in safeguards. All the bases were covered. I would remain in complete control, I would go no deeper than I wished to go, I would select for myself the past lives I wanted to experience, and I could come out of the trance state at any moment I decided to do so. Well, who could ask for more? There seemed to be nothing to lose and maybe something important to gain. So I decided to go with it.

I had absolutely no difficulty entering the trance state. As instructed, I began the eye movement/reverse counting maneuver at the count of ten. When I reached one and closed my eyes, I knew I was in deep hypnosis. I saw no need to use the finger numbness test. I immediately and with great ease regressed to the first grade where I was molding clay into an action figure.

With some apprehension, I left the first grade knowing that I was about to enter a past life. Although I knew I was in deep hypnosis, I had some difficulty with the Past-life Corridor technique. I've always been uncomfortable in enclosed places, and the thought of entering a corridor was rather threatening, and the thought of entering a small room was even more intimidating. I finally solved this problem by visualizing a very high and wide corridor with very big doors and much space between them. The corridor was so long that I could not see the doors at the end of it, though I knew they were there.

When I entered the corridor, I was totally at ease. I knew there was something to be learned here. I walked past several doors and finally came upon a steel door that somehow intrigued me. I noticed that I was for some unknown reason wearing mesh metal gloves, and when I reached out to touch the door, my glove stuck to it like a magnet. It was almost as though I expected this to happen. Although I am in this present life an engineer, I am intrigued with the possibility of magnetic healing and have reviewed some of the research related to it.

I gave the door a light push, whereupon it opened and released my hand. What I saw inside was a laboratory with an empty chair at a very long counter. I entered the laboratory as if it were my own, and as soon as I sat in the chair, I knew my identity. At that point, I became William Gilbert. In front of me were globular magnets or terrellas with magnetic needles on them pointing to the poles. I knew that I was a physicist who believed the earth to be a giant magnet with magnetic poles. I also knew that I was chief physician to Queen Elizabeth I, and that I would see her this very afternoon for irregularities in her body's monthly cycles.

When I decided to leave the room, I knew that I would be leaving my own past life behind. I looked around to find something to bring back with me as proof that I had visited my lab. I then realized that it was not possible to bring something tangible back from out of the past. Or was it? I began to look for other evidence that I could use as proof. Finally, I removed my mesh gloves and on top of my left hand I saw a small, pear shaped patch of red which I recognized as a birthmark. I thought, "This is all the evidence I need."

Leaving the metal gloves behind, I left the room, closed the door behind me, and exited the tunnel. Stopping briefly by the first-grade classroom and putting a finishing touch on the action figure, I returned to the present and exited hypnosis with ease.

I immediately examined the top of my left hand, and as expected, found no birthmark.

### Follow-on Entry:

My research of William Gilbert confirmed many of the details of my regression experience. He was a physicist whose principal discovery was that the earth is a giant magnet with magnetic poles. He was also chief physician to Queen Elizabeth I who experienced irregularities in her menstrual cycles. But one detail I could not confirm: I have not to this day found any reference to the red, pear-shaped birthmark on his left hand. I'm still searching. Hopefully, I will someday uncover this small piece of collaborative evidence.

My past-life regression experience is important to me for several reasons. First, it proved to my satisfaction that I have lived not just one but many past lifetimes—there were at least ten doors on each side of the Past-life Corridor. I'm looking forward to opening each of them. Second, the experience convinced me of my ability to regress myself and to discover for myself whatever I need to know about my past lives. Finally, the experience explained, at least to some extent, my interest in the magnetic healing, a topic I am presently researching.

I'm still somewhat uncomfortable in enclosed places. I suspect its source is another past lifetime, which I hope later to discover.

Not all regression experiences involve important past-life achievements of prominent persons. Most, in fact, do not. Nevertheless, every past-life regression experience is relevant in some way. After all, past-life experiences are a part of our past growth and they come forth during regression for a purpose.

## Subject 3: College professor, male, age 32
## Journal Entry:

I am a skeptic. I've always considered ESP, OBEs, PK, remote viewings, and especially, ghosts as for the most part, nonsense. I may have had one or two déjà vu experiences, but I explained them as physiologically based, not psychic. The human aura, in my opinion, is a visual phenomenon only. My few so-called ESP experiences I attributed to chance or imagination. I've never seen a ghost, and I still do not believe they exist.

But I've always been intrigued by the possibility of reincarnation. Nevertheless, when I decided to try past-life regression, I expected to experience either nothing or something irrelevant. But what appealed to me most was the possibility that I could myself experience hypnosis on my own without the aid of an "expert." Although I had seen hypnosis demonstrated by my instructor in a college classroom, I was not convinced that the phenomenon actually existed as a valid altered state. After all, students who need to please the instructor could fake hypnosis and possibly receive extra credit for being a "good volunteer subject." I am a bit reluctant to admit it, but I was once myself a volunteer. Unfortunately, my utter failure to respond I think may have irritated the professor and banished all possibility of any special consideration.

When I decided to try self-hypnosis, I expected, in all honesty, no credible results, but the idea of self-regression into a past life intrigued me. I would not be relying on a hypnotist I may or may not trust, and I certainly had nothing to lose by attempting something new. Although I am skeptical still, I think being open to new experiences is important, even when the promised benefits seem improbable.

When I began the EM/RC procedure, my immediate impression was, "This will not work for me." I got off to a bad start by shifting my eyes to the left on the count of ten rather than to the right. I then thought, "So what the hell, it really doesn't matter." Actually, it really didn't matter, because by the count of five, my eyes were already quite tired, and by the count of one, I could hardly shift them.

Upon closing my eyes, I felt strangely relieved—I knew I was for the first time in hypnosis. I then regressed to an early childhood experience of playing with my little brother on a beach. To my surprise, it was as though I was actually there. I even felt the ocean breeze over my body and the warm sand—almost too warm—under my feet. Turning to my left, I saw a nearby cliff with a large ledge jutting over the beach. Underneath the ledge appeared an opening leading deep into the cliff. I thought: "I can use this as my Past-life Corridor."

The cliff with its opening provided an easy transition from the childhood beach experience to the past-life corridor. I entered the opening expecting only darkness, but was met instead by multicolored illumination moving about and reminding me of the aurora borealis. Pausing at the entrance, I marveled at the indescribable beauty of the place. The floor appeared to be of polished marble and the walls of smooth ivory. The long corridor had many doors, all of which were intricately carved but with no two exactly alike.

The corridor seemed to eventually curve to the right so that I could see it only in part. I wandered what could be the significance of a winding corridor. Could it mean that my past lacked focus or that I had little sense of direction? Or that I was creative or had broken away from the pack? I then thought, "What the hell, quit speculating and open a bloody door!"

A bit impetuously, I turned to the first door at my right—a bright red, arched door with a round window like a porthole. I opened the door—somewhat cautiously I admit—only to find that the room was empty—no furnishing, curtains, tables, chairs, not even a light fixture. The walls were bare and there were no windows. Everything—walls, ceilings, floors—was white! Anyway, I decided to enter the room, and once inside, I felt only emptiness, like the room itself.

I wondered, "What can be learned from feeling empty in an empty room?" Then it occurred to me—I may have inadvertently erased a past life! Is that possible, I thought, and if so, how? Could a hollow, empty past life be somehow connected to my skepticism? Or could I be in denial of a past life? Was it so horrific that I was unable to experience it again? Perhaps I was being protected from some unspeakable past-life atrocity?

I waited, hopeful that something, anything would unfold. But nothing did. I soon began to wonder whether the other rooms in the corridor were empty, but I knew I could not open another door, not on this trip at least!

With these thoughts lingering in my mind, I left the room and closed the door behind me. From the bright corridor, I returned to the beach to play briefly again with my brother, and from there, into the present.

**Follow-on Entry:**

For some time after the regression experience, I felt empty, or more like disappointed or somehow tricked—like you'd feel if you had opened a gift but found nothing inside. I still am unsure about this experience and its significance. The whole episode was so convincing that, I admit, it must have some relevance. Did substituting the cave for the corridor have something to do with it? Could I have experienced another totally different dimension of reality? On the other hand, could certain aspects of my past life be beyond my present capacity to experience them? Could the regression experience have been a particular segment of a past-life, such as at a time of great loss? Could the barren room represent the pre-natal stage of my development, or perhaps a past life that ended pre-natally?

I have finally concluded that certain parts of my past must, at least for now, remain unknown to me. I will eventually revisit the corridor. I may even open again the red door with the round window, hopeful that its relevance will be revealed.

This subject did indeed revisit the red door with its round window as well as several other doors in his personal Past-life Corridor. Interesting, the room behind the red door remained empty, but the other doors, according to the professor, open onto a variety of past-life experiences. In one past-life, he was a star athlete, but in another more distant lifetime, he was put to death by burning during the Inquisition in Spain.

## Recent Past Lifetimes

As earlier noted, our more recent past lifetimes often seem to be more strongly related to our present lifetime. To further explore that relationship, we organized a study in which thirty volunteer subjects used the EM/RC and Past-life Corridor procedures to regress to their most recent past lifetime as represented by the door nearest to the corridor's entrance (TR 8). When we compared the descriptions of their regression experiences, a very interesting pattern emerged. With only a few exceptions, each participant of our study experienced past lifetimes with residual effects that seemed to strongly contribute to their present attitudes, beliefs, and life-goals. Here are a few examples.

- Before his regression, a twenty-seven-year-old stockbroker expressed concern that war is too often seen as a viable solution to global problems. "There is no 'good' war," he said. "We have glorified war and desensitized ourselves to its horrors. The old make war and the young die in it." During past-life regression, he experienced a recent past lifetime in which he was tortured and executed at age nineteen as a prisoner during the Vietnam War.

- A successful business owner found that, in her most recent past lifetime, she was a man who traveled westward in a wagon with his family to start a new life. Sadly, his wife died on the trail during childbirth. He and his four children eventually reached California where he started a hardware business and amassed a small fortune. Here's her description of her present life: "I believe in my ability to succeed. Despite many barriers and setbacks, I have already achieved many of my life's goals through sheer determination. Nothing can stop me once I make up my mind."

- A young woman who had leaped to her death with her lover in her most recent past lifetime reacted to the tragedy by insulating herself against falling in love in her present lifetime, or as she put it, "becoming entangled in love." She effectively distanced herself from men through her commitment to her career. As owner of a women's fitness center, she often worked up to eighteen hours daily. She noted: "My work is my life—it doesn't leave much time for anything else."

- A writer of children's books discovered a recent past lifetime which explained her combined fear of crowds and bridges. While crossing a bridge to escape a volcanic eruption, she was caught in the push of the crowd and was trampled to death.

• A thirty-six-year-old museum curator experienced a past lifetime in which he was a cave dweller. In that lifetime, which he believed to be his only past life, he resisted the killing of animals, preferring instead to remain at the cave site where his drawings on the cave wall depicted aspects of life in his primitive culture. He is today a vegetarian, animal rights activist, and collector of primitive art.

• A forty-two-year-old detective experienced a troubling past lifetime in which he was a serial killer. In that lifetime, which he considered his most recent, he went on a killing spree through several states before taking refuge in a mountain cabin where he was finally shot dead by police. His present career and commitment to law enforcement, he concluded, are efforts to expiate the residual guilt and undo the wrongs associated with his most recent past lifetime.

• A firefighter, upon regressing to his most recent past lifetime, found that he was a pyromaniac who set numerous fires before becoming a victim of his own crimes. Caught in an abandoned building after starting a blaze, he leaped to his death from the eighth floor. His present career in fire fighting, he concluded, is an effort to undo the wrongs of his most recent past lifetime. His fear of heights could be explained as the residual effects of his panic and leap to death in that lifetime. As noted earlier, many of our phobias, obsessions, and compulsions are associated with recent past-life experiences. They are almost always resolved through insight into their past-life origins, as was the case with this firefighter.

- A nineteen-year-old pre-med student believed himself to be a vampire and in fact admitted to having belonged to a vampire cult and periodically drinking vials of blood. He experienced during regression a past lifetime in which he was a physician who practiced bloodletting. With that insight, he abandoned his vampiristic practices.

- A thirty-year-old minister whose work included a prison ministry described the world as "essentially unfair" and "basically without justice." According to him, "Many innocent people go to prison, and many guilty people do not. There are innocent people on death row, and some of them will probably be executed." During regression, he experienced a past lifetime in which he was a prisoner held in solitary confinement before being finally executed for a crime he did not commit.

Our past-life experiences can be so intense that awareness of them not only alters our perceptions, but brings forth profound changes in our behavior as well. If we are indeed the totality of all our past experiences, most of which remain beyond conscious awareness, it would seem only reasonable that many potentially empowering experiences are among them. To uncover them and activate their powers could literally change the directions of our lives. Conceivably, they could provide solutions to pressing problems, and explain behaviors that would otherwise mystify us. At a deeply personal level, my discovery of a very intense past-life experience did just that! Here's what happened.

It all started in my office at Athens State University on a very cold, rainy winter afternoon during a discussion with several of my colleagues who were assisting with a research project I was at the time conducting for the U.S. Army. We were having sassafras tea, one of my favorite beverages, when I began to experience a series of very subtle déjà vu impressions, which I at first associated with childhood memories of digging up sassafras roots and my mother brewing tea from them on an old wood stove. But as the impressions persisted and, in fact, grew stronger, I began to suspect they were past-life related.

Leaving my colleagues to discuss the research project among themselves, I withdrew to my inner office with its comfortable fainting couch. Using the EM/RC and Past-life Corridor as developed for the study then in progress, I induced a trance state, regressed to childhood, and entered with ease the past-life corridor as I had done several times before in search of information concerning my past lifetimes.

When I entered the corridor, a door to my right instantly commanded my attention with a brilliance I had not seen before. Although I had barely noticed it in my previous regressions, the door now stood out above all the others in the corridor of many doors. It was an elegantly designed door that suggested both formality and hospitality.

I approached the door hesitantly, knowing it held something significant but questioning my readiness to experience it. I placed my hand against the door, whereupon it flung fully open to reveal an elaborately decorated Victorian parlor with, incidentally, a fainting couch. Upon entering the room, I found myself, a man in my twenties, having sassafras tea with my fiancée and a small group of friends. It was a cold, rainy afternoon. I recognized the setting as my fiancée's home around the mid-1800s. The conversation had turned to political issues, a topic of little interest to me though of considerable concern to others present.

As the afternoon wore on, I took my leave around dusk for the horseback ride to my home. With the group gathered on the front porch of the tall brick house, I mounted my horse and rode down a tree-lined lane, shielding my face with my arm from the driving rain. Upon approaching a shallow stream, my horse suddenly reared at a loud clap of thunder, throwing me forcefully into the stream where my head struck a rock.

Injured and unable to move, I felt myself leaving my body to view from above an unfolding series of events. I saw several men rushing from the house to pull me from the stream. I watched as I was carried inside and placed on the fainting couch where I was pronounced dead. A mirror held close to my face to detect breathing confirmed it.

I then found myself back in my body, but still could neither move nor open my eyes, no matter how hard I tried. I wondered, "Can I really be dead? How could I be dead and still think I am alive? How could I be dead and still know what's happening?"

I remained in that state for what seemed hours. Finally I was prepared for burial and placed in a roughly hand-hewn coffin. As time wore on, I endured my own funeral, which seemed too long, still trying desperately to move or communicate that I was not dead. Finally, the casket was closed and taken to a gravesite where, in total darkness, I felt myself being unsteadily lowered into the grave. I heard the shoveling of earth and the muffled sound of dirt mixed with rock striking the casket until all that remained was darkness and silence. Finally, I was able to move a hand, then an arm, and eventually both legs. In panic, I pushed my knees against the hand-hewn coffin lid, its splinters digging into my flesh. Then in relief, I felt myself once again leaving my body.

Suddenly, I became aware of the past-life door, still half-open to reveal the bright corridor outside. I quickly returned to the corridor and closed the door behind me.

Relieved at being once again in the corridor, I returned to the present. Reflecting on the experience, I was at once reminded of my fear of enclosed places. I had experienced the fear for the first time as a child while playing indoor hide-and-seek with my two brothers. Hiding on my back under a bed, I had discovered in panic that I could neither move nor speak. What's more, I could hardly breathe, no matter how hard I tried. I was literally paralyzed with fear as what seemed to be an intolerable, immovable weight pressed down upon my chest. I had never heard of the near-death experience, but I thought, "This is it." Finally at what seemed to have been the last second of my life, my brothers pulled me by my feet from under the bed. From that point forward, I avoided all enclosed places.

In my efforts to overcome the ever-persistent fear, I tried for myself the same conventional techniques I had used with my patients—all based on the theory that phobias are learned responses and therefore extinguishable. The theory is sound and the strategies are often effective, but for me they had failed.

Had I finally discovered through past-life regression the source of my fear of enclosed places? It seemed reasonable to me that being buried alive in a past life could result in fear of enclosed places in a present lifetime. Would past-life knowledge finally bring success in my efforts to overcome a lifelong fear? I checked the time—my regression experience had taken only thirty minutes, though it had seemed much longer. I rejoined my colleagues who were still drinking sassafras tea and ironically, speculation on whether reincarnation is fact or fiction! "Where's the evidence for it?" one colleague asked. Another replied, "Where's the evidence against it?" Finally, the debate ended with apparently no shifting of opinions.

Later that day, I decided to test the effects of my regression experience on my long-term fear of enclosed places. For the first time in my adult life, I slid under my bed and while lying on my back, felt absolutely no fear. I was relaxed and breathing normally. My fear of enclosed places had been extinguished once and for all! I had discovered for myself the liberating power of past-life enlightenment.

## *Other Lifetimes, Other Beings*

The human form as we know it is probably not the only mode for the embodiment of souls. While it may seem far-fetched, it is plausible that we could have lived past lifetimes on another planet in a distant galaxy or even in another universe as other intelligent beings. To restrict our embodiment to the human form on this planet would eliminate a vast range of important growth possibilities. Some of our subjects during regression did, in fact, experience past lifetimes on other planets in different animated forms.

Our very recent studies that probed the afterlife also suggested the possibility of past lifetimes on earth in other life forms (TR 31). Knowing what it's like to exist as another life form could be important to our evolution as souls. My life-long love of birds suggests to my satisfaction that I may have been a bird in a past life as an essential part of my evolvement. Knowing what it was like to be embodied as a bird could explain my strong interest in bird watching today and my great appreciation of these beautiful beings. Beyond that, I don't rule out the possibility of having existed as some other living creature. Raised on a farm, I often checked the horses' watering troughs as a child to rescue insects that had fallen into the water. Upon once rescuing a near-drowned moth, I held the fragile insect briefly in my hand to let it recover and then watched it as it took flight. Suddenly, it occurred to me that possibly I had been a moth in a past life, and that maybe someone had rescued me. I thought that perhaps it was important for me to experience what it was like to have been a moth, or if not a moth, perhaps a grasshopper or cricket in a past lifetime. If not an insect, possibly a tree—I always thought of myself as a tree person. I became convinced early on that experiencing life in other living forms could help us to appreciate the value of all living things.

## *The Numbers Question*

Most of us have probably speculated on how many past lifetimes we may have lived. We know, of course, that a higher number of past lifetimes alone does not necessarily signify greater quality of growth. Although many past lifetimes would seem to suggest many growth opportunities, it's important to keep in mind that a single lifetime of focused growth can be of far greater importance to our evolvement than many lifetimes of missed opportunities. It's also important to keep in mind that we bring into each new lifetime not only the experiences of our past lifetimes, but our experiences between them as well. Fewer lifetimes could suggest a greater repository of between-lifetimes experiences. Even the person with no past-lifetime experience could be richly endowed with preexistence experiences.

As an aside, it's important again to note that the life span of souls is endless, with neither beginning nor end. Consequently, souls have no "chronological age" and the number of past lifetimes one has lived has absolutely no age relevance.

Although the quantity of past lifetimes may have questionable relevance to the quality of our evolvement, we know that each lifetime is purposeful and rich in new growth possibilities. A major objective of any past-life regression effort is to uncover those experiences from out of our past that hold relevance to our present growth. Discovering the total number of your past lifetimes could be pertinent to your search, with each past lifetime being a marker suggesting a new body of enlightenment possibilities.

Here are four strategies you can use to discover the total number of your past lifetimes:

1.  During your past-life regression using the Past-life Corridor, count the number of past-lifetime doors in the corridor. If your present lifetime is your first, the corridor will have neither a past-lifetime door nor a life-between-life-

times door. It will have only the preexistence door at the corridor's end.

2. Directly ask your subconscious. All your past-life experiences, including those that exist beyond conscious awareness, remain forever a part of your being. Fortunately, your subconscious is a willing collaborator, always receptive to your conscious probes. For this simple procedure, clear your mind, and with your eyes closed, ask yourself, "How many past lifetimes have I lived?" The number that spontaneously comes to mind is your subconscious response. That number is more reliable than any other number that may afterward surface due to conscious reasoning.

3. Use automatic writing. Like the above, this procedure is based on the premise that your past-life experiences are stored in your subconscious and receptive to your probes. For this simple procedure, all you need is a blank sheet of paper and a writing pen or pencil. With the point of your pen or pencil resting lightly on the sheet of paper, close your eyes and clear your mind. In your own words, state your objective of discovering through automatic writing the number of past lifetimes you have lived. Then allow automatic writing to occur spontaneously, totally independent of any effort on your part. The number that eventually comes forth is often preceded by certain warm-up scribbling or drawing. Allow plenty of time for the number representing the sum of your past lifetimes to spontaneously emerge.

4. Use your body's antennae—the index finger of either hand —as a dowsing tool to unlock your subconscious and uncover the number of your past lifetimes. The key words here are "unlock" and "uncover." The answer exists within yourself, but it's up to you to unlock your subconscious

and uncover the information. For this strategy, use a numbers table which includes vertical columns of numbers starting at 0. At the end of each column is a space without a number which indicates the scan is to continue from the top of the next column as indicated. You can make your own numbers table or use the Past-Lifetime Chart shown on page 69.

Start the procedure by taking in a few deep breaths and relaxing your body from your head downward. Clear your mind of active thought and then place the index fingertip of either hand lightly on the space above 0. Affirm that your fingertip as it moves downward will come to rest on the number that signifies the sum total of your past lifetimes. Scan slowly downward with your finger gently touching the table until it stops on a number. Here is the complete Past-Lifetime Chart.

## Past-Lifetime Chart

This chart is designed to identify the sum total of your past lifetimes. Place the index fingertip of either hand on the space preceding 0, and with your fingertip gently touching the page, affirm that as you scan downward, your finger will come to rest on the number that signifies the sum total of your past lifetimes. At the end of each column is a space that indicates the scan is to continue from the top of the next column. The space at the end of the last column indicates that the scan is to continue from the top of the first column to determine the number of additional lifetimes. Continue the scan until your finger comes to rest.

## Reincarnation in the Laboratory

Over many years, reincarnation has been the topic of research in our laboratory. Among our earliest projects was a study for the U.S.

___(Start Here)

| 0 | | |
|---|---|---|
| 1 | 11 | 21 |
| 2 | 12 | 22 |
| 3 | 13 | 23 |
| 4 | 14 | 24 |
| 5 | 15 | 25 |
| 6 | 16 | 26 |
| 7 | 17 | 27 |
| 8 | 18 | 28 |
| 9 | 19 | 29 |
| 10 | 20 | 30 |
| ___(Go to next column) | ___(Go to next column) | ___(Go to first column) |

Army which was designed to investigate the human energy system and its relationship to various mental states (TR 4). Using Kirlian electrophotography to record the aura energy patterns surrounding the index fingertip, the study found a strong relationship between the energy patterns and certain mental states. A follow-on study funded by the Parapsychology Foundation of New York further investigated electrophotography with particular emphasis on its usefulness in monitoring certain altered states, including hypnosis and age regression (TR 9).

Together, these studies along with our follow-on research found that both brightness and magnitude of the aura decreased with the introduction of hypnosis using the EM/RC self-induction procedure (TR 20). Upon regression to childhood, the decrease continued, a phenomenon we called the "image decline effect." Upon regression to past-life using the Past-life Corridor, however, the brightness and magnitude of the aura dramatically increased, a phenomenon we called "past-life illumination." Finally, upon regression to preexistence, the increase in brightness and magnitude of the

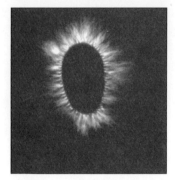

A

B

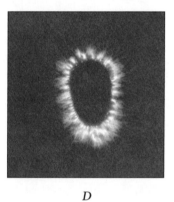

C

D

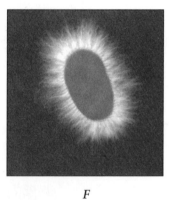

E

F

*Figure 2. Kirlian Electrophotographs for Six Conditions:*
*(A) No Treatment, (B) Hypnosis, (C) Age Regression to Childhood,*
*(D) Past-life Regression, (E) Preexistence Regression,*
*and (F) Life-between-Lifetimes Regression.*

aura was even greater, a phenomenon we called "preexistence en-lightenment." For life-between-lifetimes, the aura pattern remained basically the same as for preexistence (see figure 2).

The findings of this research were important to our regression studies for several reasons. First, they validated the usefulness of aura photography in monitoring certain altered states of con-sciousness; second, they showed a relationship between the aura and certain altered states; third, they indicated the uniqueness of the different states being studied; and finally, they validated the ef-fectiveness of EM/RC and Past-life Corridor as past-life regression procedures.

In our lab studies using electrophotography to record aura en-ergies, we often noted an energy image outside the normal range of aura activity. This pattern, which we called "remote image," seems to suggest the presence of a spirit guide or other benevolent influ-ence. This interesting pattern was noted in the photo of a student

*Figure 3. Remote Image Phenomenon.*
*Note the subdued image outside the normal range of aura energy activity.*

who earlier in the day had narrowly avoided a serious auto accident. When he saw the image in his photo for the first time, he said: "That's my guardian angel!" (See figure 3.)

Based on these and other studies, we continue to use electrophotography in our labs to monitor various altered states and develop effective procedures for inducing them.

## *Summary*

Through past-life regression using strategies such as EM/RC and Past-life Corridor, you can both observe and interact with your personal past. As either a spectator or active participant, you can experience important events that made up your past history as an evolving soul. You can become empowered to retrieve past-life experiences that hold particular relevance to your present development.

All your past-life experiences exist within yourself—they are a part of your evolution as a soul. By tapping into them, you can reactivate the growth potentials of your past experiences and integrate them into your soul being where they function as new growth resources.

In probing your past life, you may find that an unresolved conflict or phobia is directly past-life related. Fortunately, past-life enlightenment is often sufficient in and of itself to resolve present conflicts and extinguish distressful phobias which otherwise could constrict our present growth. Not surprisingly, your past-life experiences often provided solutions to present life problems while motivating and inspiring us to reach higher levels of spiritual growth.

Your past-life experiences and the enlightenment based on them contribute to your uniqueness as an evolving soul while offering resources with permanent growth possibilities. Because souls exist forever—they have neither a beginning nor an ending—the destiny of souls is for growth and greatness, from everlasting to everlasting. You are an immortal spirit entity whose identity remains forever unchanged and whose evolvement is forever continuous.

As emphasized throughout this book, the soul, rather than something you possess, is what you are. It is that unique eternal essence—the "I am" of your being that sets you apart from all other beings.

It is important to celebrate differences among souls—differences in interests, abilities, achievements, backgrounds, and so forth. But it is also important to keep in mind that we have a common attribute—that of forever evolving—which makes us more alike than different. That attribute can promote tolerance and acceptance of others. It can facilitate communication and understanding between widely different cultures. It can help unite us in our efforts to achieve global peace and make the world a better place for ourselves and future generations.

We can now conclude with reasonable certainty that past-life knowledge is power in one of its purest forms.

*A moment's insight is sometimes worth a life's experience.*
—Oliver Wendell Holmes, Sr., "Iris, Her Book,"
The Professor at the Breakfast Table (1860)

# 4

# PREEXISTENCE AND
# LIFE-BETWEEN-LIFETIMES

As souls, we evolve within a life span that is from everlasting to everlasting. Growth without end is our destiny. But if we are to understand the full scope of our existence, we must examine the different dimensions of our lives and their interrelationships.

We have already explored those very critical intervals known as our past lifetimes using the EM/RC and Past-life Corridor. We have focused particularly on the relevance of past lifetimes to our present existence. We have illustrated the enlightenment and healing potentials of our past-life experiences when integrated into our present lifetimes.

We will now examine two additional dimensions of our past existence: (1) our preexistence before our first lifetime and (2) our existence between lifetimes. In exploring these critical aspects of our past, it is again important to note that our existence is not only forever, it is forever forward.

## *Preexistence*

Because of the infinite magnitude of our past, probes of our preexistence are typically more productive when they focus on relevance rather than scope. Given such a focused probe, we can then integrate our preexistence into our present lifetime experiences. Fortunately, there exists within each of us an inner knowing, which we could call our higher or super consciousness, with power to ferret out those crucial experiences from our past and reveal their present relevance. Beyond that, we have access to the spirit world with all its powerful resources poised to enrich our search.

In probing your past life, either as an observer or active participant, it is important to keep in mind that the spirit dimension is not some distant mystery realm, but rather a present and receptive reality. It is as close to you right now as the air you breathe. As a soul, you are interconnected to that dimension. You have within yourself the power to reach out at any moment to touch and directly interact with it. Through regression, you can re-discover the spirit realm as you experienced it before your first lifetime as well as between your past lifetimes. In chapter 5 we will explore techniques and tools for experiencing the spirit realm as it exists in the present.

## *Exploring Preexistence*

Over the years, scores of subjects participating in our past-life regression studies volunteered to explore their preexistence (TR 16, TR 18, TR 19). To uncover their past, they used the EM/RC and Past-life Corridor procedures as previously discussed to induce hypnosis and then enter the Past-life Corridor. To experience their preexistence, they opened the preexistence door at the end of the corridor and observed their preexistence as a spectator from the open doorway. From there, many of them chose to step through the doorway to become active participants in their preexistence as they knew it before their first lifetime on earth. Our journey back to our preexistence is, of course, a journey within ourselves in which we discover anew the vastness of our past and how it relates to our present and future.

Upon opening the door to their preexistence, the subjects of our studies were struck with awe at its magnificence and orderliness. Such descriptions as *took my breath away, unbelievably beautiful, truly a paradise,* and *absolutely gorgeous* were not unusual. Our spectator subjects described the beauty of their preexistence as beyond anything they had even experienced in physical reality. They were met with a panoramic view of indescribable splendor stretching out before them.

Without exception, our subjects were astonished at the magnificent variety of sights and sounds characterizing their preexistence. Many of them experienced the wondrous sounds of music, which came as no surprise since music is the magical language that unites us all. One subject, a student majoring in music, noted: "It was like playing a violin—I felt the vibrations under my skin." Typically, our subjects felt instantly attuned to their preexistence and the energies that infused them.

As spectators, they saw shimmering planes of beauty stretching endlessly into the distance, sometimes as glowing streams like molten glass. One of our subjects described it as similar to a moon-lit landscape with fluid-like forms and radiant colors that span the color spectrum. They were impressed by the orderly configuration of multiple planes. Several subjects who had been trained in out-of-body travel to the spirit realm recognized certain planes they had already visited during astral projection (see my book *Astral Projection and Psychic Empowerment*). In their previous out-of-body experiences, they had interacted with cosmic planes of different colors and energy frequencies. They had discovered the rejuvenating and healing

properties of brilliant emerald planes, the intellectual and enlightenment properties of bright yellow planes, the serenity and peaceful properties of sparkling blue planes, and the inspirational quali-
ties of deep purple planes.

For our subjects who had been trained in aura viewing, the radiant colors characterizing preexistence planes were similar to
those observed in the human aura (see my book *Aura Energy for
Health, Healing & Balance*). One of our subjects, a student who is
color blind, saw color for the first time upon opening the door to
his preexistence. He was struck not only by the wondrous beauty of
the colors but by what he called the color music and sound har-
monies they radiated.

From their vantage point as spectators at the doorway to their
preexistence, the participants in our studies were moved by the perfect symmetry and balance of the realm's design. They observed vibrant structural forms including orbs, domes, mountain-like for-
mations, and arches reminiscent of the rainbow. One of our
subjects, a marine biologist, observed shimmering streams, lakes,
and rivers of energy teeming with marine life forms. I am a tree person and bird watcher so I was not surprised during my own preexistence regression to see a dense primeval forest with splendid trees,
lush undergrowth, and magnificent feathered beings as showy and
colorful as the macaw. Though probably discounted as fantasy by
some, the experience for me was an unforgettable, inspiring reality.

Aside from the spectacular beauty of the preexistence realm,
our subjects were profoundly affected by the realm's human spirit
entities. They recognized human spirit entities as radiant beings
who were actively engaged in gaining wisdom, sharing knowledge,
and nurturing the growth of each other. According to our subjects,
souls existed in diverse forms, but all were seen as bright beings
with the capacity for growth and change. They emitted vibrant energy in its finest form. They were seen as embodying thoughts,
memories, and emotions, while always radiating knowledge and

love. Every soul was seen as an excellent work in progress, arrayed in beauty, and full of life. As we will later see, souls with past lifetimes integrated all their past-life experiences into an upward spiral of endless growth.

Our subjects, even as spectators, experienced their preexistence as "a fellowship of friends." As souls, they interacted with each other, including souls with past lifetimes. They learned about life on earth, often experiencing it vicariously. They viewed earth events from a distance and sometimes interacted with incarnates. Several of our subjects reported that during their preexistence, they had worked together with other souls, some with past lifetimes, to influence earth happenings. Though the specifics of those interventions were not always clear, they seemed always directed toward positive outcomes. In some instances, souls as groups worked together to generate vibrations that influenced world events.

As spectators of their preexistence, our subjects sensed no need for a hierarchy of power or preoccupation with status—oneness and harmony prevailed everywhere. Although they saw great diversity among souls and their growth levels, our subjects saw no inferior or imperfect souls—every soul was seen as a being of incomparable worth and beauty. They witnessed many manifestations of love, caring, and affection throughout the preexistence realm. Although souls varied in their growth levels, there existed no stereotyping or classifying of souls based on their evolvement or any other soul attribute. While individual differences among souls were recognized and valued, the similarity and oneness of souls were emphasized. Though it may seem overly idealistic, growth goals among souls in their preexistence were always toward evolvement and fulfillment, both for themselves and others.

According to our subjects, judgment, punishment, guilt, and suffering are unknown in the preexistence realm (TR 44). Relationships, roles, and functions among souls were growth and enlightenment oriented. Among the common activities were learning by discovery and interaction, including interacting with incarnates on the earth plane, a phenomenon we will later explore.

It is interesting to note that upon viewing their preexistence, our subjects reported seeing darkness and light as existing separately but in ways that complemented each other. The common practice of associating darkness with evil was rejected by all our regression subjects. There exists, according to our subjects, absolutely no place for evil in the preexistence realm. They saw darkness as essential to light and light as essential to darkness. In general, they concluded that darkness and light are the complementary essentials of consciousness, with darkness signifying potential yet to be developed and light signifying potential already developed—together, they interact in ways that are fundamental to the evolution of the spirit. None of our subjects came away from the regression experience believing that evil characterized in any way the preexistence of souls.

Our subjects described their preexistence as without borders or the familiar constrictions of time and space. The spirit realm with its magnificent planes and other forms stretched endlessly with a beauty that could not be described. Simply to view it was a peak experience for our subjects.

Our subjects, upon stepping into their preexistence to become active participants, experienced an infusion of pure energy and a state of peace beyond anything they had experienced in their present lifetime. They experienced complete autonomy, along with harmony and equality with all other souls, a state many of them described as a collective oneness within which they felt connected to all other souls while at the same time, maintaining their own individuality and full personal cosmic identity. They experienced unconditional love as the preeminent characteristic of collective oneness. According to them, it is unconditional love that sustains all that exists, both physical and spiritual (TR 42).

In their preexistence (and as we will later see in afterlife as well), all souls seem to experience no limits in their ability to recognize other souls. They found that all souls had a personality identity by which they were known. They recognized each other by their flawless cosmic makeup or spiritual genotype. Within that perfect cosmic makeup, they had the ability to assume a variety of observable energy forms. For souls with a past lifetime, that ability included the capacity to assume in spirit form the physical features of that embodiment. The ability of souls in the spirit realm to assume a past recognizable form, of course, could facilitate their interactions with souls left behind. The many appearances of recognizable spirits or ghosts of the departed are familiar examples of that capacity, as we will see in chapter 5.

Strange as it might at first appear, our regression studies found that souls retained the capacity to assume the physical appearance of not only their most recent past embodiment but any past lifetime they had lived (TR 27). For example, Lincoln's ghost is still seen at the White House although our research suggests that Lincoln has lived at least one other more recent lifetime—that of a physician. His life as Lincoln, however, remains within his repertoire of past lifetimes. His intermittent appearance as Lincoln in ghost form appears to be for him a fond reminiscence of a past lifetime that helped shape history.

In their interactions with other souls, preincarnates as well as souls with past lifetimes had perfect command of a "spiritual or cosmic language." They communicated, exchanged ideas, expressed emotions, explored challenging new concepts, and experienced love in its purest form. Their thought processes were free and uninhibited. They learned from each other. Always, they felt a comfortable oneness with all souls, whether other preincarnates or souls with past lifetimes.

Repeatedly, our regression subjects described their preexistence as a place of perfect peace and harmony (TR 16). They experienced a love state called authentic love, which seemed to be the central, unifying force of the preexistence realm. They recognized neither superior nor inferior souls. While acknowledging differences in growth levels among souls, they found excellence, equality, and value to be among the essential characterizes of all souls. Their interactions with other souls were characterized by understanding, affection, and unconditional positive regard. Although these conditions may seem almost too good to be true, our subjects found them to be absolutely essential to their preexistence. They found absolutely no place for insecurity, inferiority, or anything harmful in the preexistence realm.

According to many of our subjects, the most impressive structural features of the preexistence realm were the so-called "cosmic gardens" which included wondrous fountains and shimmering pools of what seemed to be the highest forms of energy. They described bathing in the spray of these fountains as "therapy for the soul." Diving into the shimmering pools was "sheer ecstasy" from which they emerged fully energized, attuned, and balanced. Situated among the many colorful planes, these gardens were seen by our subjects as "beautiful classrooms for the soul" in which they grew in wisdom and power before their first lifetime on earth (and later, between lifetimes).

It was usually in these garden settings that our subjects interacted with master teachers and guides, some of whom had lived past lifetimes on earth and in some instances, past lifetimes on other planets as well (TR 42). From ministering teachers and guides, they learned of the potential value of life on earth, along with the possible pitfalls and risks of embodiment. They examined the nature of the mind, body, and spirit interaction. They studied the nature of the spiritual and physical world, to include ways in which they interacted with each other. Under the guidance of master teachers, their learning experiences included actual observations of earth conditions and events, along with limited participation in earth affairs.

Some of our regression subjects reported having actively participated in activities that literally altered earth events. These interventions were meticulously calculated to promote the common
good. They were implemented in ways that neither interrupted balance nor generated undesired consequences of any kind.

A major feature of their preexistence development, according to
our subjects, was the discovery of their complete autonomy and
uniqueness as spirit beings along with their interconnected oneness
with the spirit world. They learned the essential principles of life
and spiritual growth. They learned to appreciate the value of souls.
They experienced themselves and others as "independent entities"
and "recognizable spirit beings" of dignity and incomparable worth.

Autonomy with guidance from highly evolved souls and teachers characterized their preexistence development. None of our subjects felt that their behavior had been shaped or controlled in any
way by others during their preexistence. In their preexistent state,
they rejected any comparisons of soul differences in worth or value.
They rejected the concept of "higher souls," preferring instead the
concept of "higher evolved souls."

Many of our regressed subjects who re-experienced their preexistence described their first impressions as similar to the lucid
dreamed. Others, particularly those who had been trained in astral
projection, compared the experience to out-of-body travel. In their
regressed state, they traveled freely among preexistent planes by intent alone. (As an aside, following their past-life regression experience, many of our subjects began using self-hypnosis and the Past-
life Corridor as a vehicle for entering the out-of-body state. Once in
the out-of-body state, they left the corridor to travel to selected destinations, which could be either terrestrial or other worlds. Upon
completion of the travel experience, they returned to the corridor
and full reengagement of the body.)

For certain of our subjects whose backgrounds included the
near-death experience, stepping into their preexistence paralleled

in some ways that experience, including sensations of being flooded with a clear soft light as their past existence stretched out before them.

Having left their post as spectators to actively engage in their preexistence, our subjects invariably reported a strong connection to the preexistence dimension. Several of our subjects described it as a "homecoming." They experienced complete freedom from the physical constrictions of life on earth. They described their instant command of "cosmic language" as an unrestricted communication skill similar to mind-to-mind communication. They readily engaged other intelligent entities, often interacting with them and communicating through the prevailing cosmic language. They experienced the ability to travel at will throughout our known universe and beyond. They reported the unlimited ability to experience close up any distant physical reality, not only as observers but also as active participants.

Observing and interacting with incarnates on the earth plane were among the major growth activities of their preexistence. They concluded that one's embodiment on earth (and other planets as well) promotes not only one's own development and ideally the development of fellow incarnates, but also the development of preexistent souls who observe and interact with incarnates. The earth, as it turns out, is a learning laboratory not only for incarnates, but for preincarnates as well. It follows that our existence in each lifetime should facilitate our own evolution as well as the evolution of others, including souls on the other side.

Many of our subjects emerged from their regression experience convinced that they had interacted with animal beings that also preexisted in spirit form. One subject, a student who worked part-time at a zoo, interacted with the spirit forms of the exotic animals like those he tended. Another student who helped raise horses interacted with the spirit forms of horses more beautiful, by his report, than any he had ever seen. Perhaps not surprising, dog owners often interacted with dogs and cat owners often interacted with cats. As we will later see, many of our subjects who regressed to their life-be-tween-lifetimes also experienced interactions with animals.

Several of our subjects reported that they had existed in non-human animal form, which included being a temporary animal walk-in as well as having lived a full lifetime on earth as an animal. The experience, rather than a stepping stone or preparation for a human incarnation, was seen instead as an important part of their evolution. For them, existing in non-human animal form was en-lightening and profoundly empowering in and of itself. They left that lifetime with a deeper understanding and appreciation of all living beings. They viewed non-human animal forms, not as lower or inferior beings, but spiritual beings of dignity and worthy of human respect. Our regression subjects who had lived as animals in a past life believed that all souls could benefit from incarnations as animals.

Several of our preexistence regression subjects reported that prior to their first incarnation, they were walk-ins of another form —they temporarily inhabited certain inanimate objects of nature. This was seen by many of our subjects as an important part of their preincarnate learning. One of our subjects, for instance, reported having inhabited a tree because, by his admission, "I've always revered trees as earth's oldest and largest living things. I wanted to learn what it was like to be a tree."

Many of our subjects believed that they had interacted during their preexistence with beings they described as angels, though the lines separating ministering spirits, guides, teachers, and angels were often blurred. All were highly evolved (rather than superior) beings who were committed to helping other souls achieve a higher level of growth.

Once inside the preexistence realm, all our subjects reported traveling at will to various planes of color and drawing revitalizing energies from them. They considered their interactions with these energy planes as a vital part of their preparation for a lifetime on earth. Also critical to their future incarnations were their interactions with their preincarnate teachers and guides, whom they perceived as dynamic, loving beings. They reported that the very presence of these being was profoundly empowering, and their interactions with them were always enlightening.

During their preexistence regression, our subjects interacted with many souls, no two of whom were described as exactly alike. Some of them had never been incarnated whereas others had lived many past lifetimes. Among their preexistence teachers were many highly evolved entities with no past-lifetime experience on this earth plane.

In their preexistence state, almost all our subjects reported they were a "soul among many souls," all with unique, identifying characteristics. They recognized diversity as an essential feature of the spirit world. Differences in soul traits were recognized and valued. An endless variety of soul traits reflected those differences. Although our subjects observed a variety of what they called soul forms, the identity and uniqueness of each soul remained stable. All the subjects in our regression studies were comfortable assuming the soul state which characterized their preexistence. They reported a sense of freedom and independence as preincarnates, while at the same time they recognized the importance of earth-plane embodiment and the growth opportunities it offered.

Our preexistence regression subjects who were trained in aura viewing often described the spirit beings with whom they interacted as enveloped in a beautiful, colorful glow similar to the human aura. One theory has it that the external aura is but an external manifestation of an internal energy core, which together manifest the spiritual nature of our being. Having observed during regression a myriad of glowing spirit forms, many of our subjects concluded that the aura as typically seen does indeed manifest the inner life force that energizes our existence as souls. Not all of our subjects agreed, however, with that perspective. Some of them reported a distant light source which they speculated may have energized the preincarnate realm, including its many planes, fountains, and pools of energy. They speculated that it may have been the source of energy for souls. Typically, however, our subjects believed that souls were energized primarily from within, thus requiring no outer energy source. While some of our subjects speculated that the light source could have been God, others insisted that God exists within the soul, not outside it.

Our regression subjects who stepped into their preexistence always recognized themselves as conscious beings with power to travel into the far reaches of the preexistence world, which was seen as having no boundaries. They reported the ability to recognize other souls as well as familiar guides and teachers with whom they communicated freely—always with unconditional love and acceptance. None of our subjects felt alienated during their journey into their preexistence.

Although our subjects found many highly evolved souls in the preexistence realm with no history of incarnation, they usually concluded that life on earth could accelerate their evolution. Here are some examples of the specific benefits of embodiment of souls as reported by our subjects immediately following their preexistence regression:

1. Each lifetime offers totally new mind, body, and spirit interactions that can promote our evolution while contributing to the evolution of others.

2. Each lifetime offers new opportunities to experience earth-plane realities and to make the world a better place.

3. Each lifetime can be a source of personal enlightenment and enrichment, including self-discovery and self-fulfillment.

4. Each lifetime expands our opportunities to experience love, commitment, and understanding of others.

5. Our earth-plane existence can build feelings of worth and well-being so essential to our continued development.

6. Earth-plane interactions expand our perspective of life and our appreciation of diversity.

7. Through our earth-plane existence, we can learn to take responsibility for the consequences of our decisions, actions, attitudes, and beliefs.

8. Each lifetime offers new opportunities to develop our nurturing, caring side. For instance, by helping others or coming to the aid of an animal in distress, we experience the fulfillment that comes only from acts of kindness.

9. Each lifetime offers opportunities to discover the beauty and power of nature.

10. Each lifetime offers opportunities for overcoming physical limitations, compensating for past actions, completing unfinished tasks, and setting new goals.

Without exception, our preexistence regression subjects reported that earth-plane embodiment was by choice; it was never imposed upon souls—that would be contrary to the very nature of souls as self-determining beings. They believed that, even in their preincarnate state of evolution, they were free agents with power to make choices, set goals, and determine their own destinies. The results are higher motivation and a greater willingness to assume responsibility for one's life and the consequences of one's actions. According to them, a lifetime on earth as a penalty or sentence would be counterproductive. Although the subjects of our studies concluded that growth is best when it is self-directed, they welcomed the continuing support of their ministering guides and teachers.

While all our subjects concluded that their embarkation to a lifetime on earth was autonomous, they recognized the importance of accompanying spirit guides throughout their lifetimes. Spirit guides, however, were never "assigned"; instead they voluntarily accompanied individuals who embarked on a lifetime, with the interaction between the guide and incarnate promoting the evolution of both.

According to our preexistence subjects, deciding to embark on an earth lifetime is a process that combines self-examination and collective interactions with other souls (TR 42). The process is informal and without imposed rules and regulations. In fact, the process which they commonly called "incarnate preparation" is a developmental phenomenon in and of itself. The preparation process is always flexible and self-initiated, and it can be abandoned or placed on hold at any time. Nothing in the preexistence realm is irreversible. Growth and progress are spontaneous and self-initiated within the scope of unlimited resources, including the wisdom and guidance of higher teachers and ministering guides.

Although our subjects agreed in principal on the nature of the preparation process involved for entering the human body, they did not all agree on the exact point of embodiment. While almost all our subjects believed that they voluntarily entered the human body at some point during prenatal development, a few believed that embodiment occurred at birth, and a very small number believed the point of embodiment to be essentially random, that is it could occur at various points during prenatal development. None of our subjects believed embodiment occurred at the union of the egg and sperm. For all of our subjects, union of the soul and body was seen as a spiritual phenomenon that signals the beginning of a new lifetime.

As it turns out, the views of our subjects concerning the point of embodiment were strongly related to their positions regarding abortion. Generally, our subjects who were opposed to abortion saw embodiment as an early prenatal event; whereas those favoring abortion rights saw embodiment as occurring later on.

Although our regression subjects' views concerning the point of origin of their existence as souls showed wide ranging differences before their regression experiences, they concluded unanimously following regression that their existence was without beginning or end. (It is important to point out again that no effort was made at any time during our studies to influence our subjects' views.) Without exception, our subjects concluded that their lifetimes on earth were "developmental intervals" which included opportunities to accelerate their personal growth while contributing to the greater good. Achieving important personal and humanitarian goals, they concluded, could require numerous lifetimes.

Here's a summary of some of our findings regarding preexistence based on the reports of scores of subjects of varying backgrounds and personal characteristics who volunteered for our studies:

1. Our existence as souls has neither seminal origin nor final destiny. The life span of every soul is endless. Before our first embodiment, it extended forever into the past; following our last embodiment, it will extend forever into the future.

2. The progress of souls in preexistence was forever forward. As in each lifetime, preexistence growth was continuous but uneven. There were periods of rapid growth and slow growth. Although growth plateaus and occasional downward spirals were observed, they were important because they prepared souls for major leaps forward. Neither so-called "arrested growth" nor "reversed growth" seemed to occur in the developmental history of souls when viewed in its totality. Growth of the soul was regulated by self-determination rather than by others.

3. All the resources required for our growth was available to us in our preexistence. Included were the collective sup-

port and wisdom of teachers and guides along with the many wondrous planes and structures—including fountains and gardens of indescribable beauty.

4. Censure, punishment, and value judgments were absent in preexistence. All souls were recognized as autonomous beings of incomparable worth and dignity. As one of our subjects put it, "I recognized certain entities as highly evolved, but equality and oneness rather than rank prevailed."

5. During their preexistence, our subjects interacted with many souls, including some who had previously lived on earth.

6. During their preexistence, our subjects occasionally interacted with souls presently living on earth. Occasionally, they intervened in earth affairs to influence unfolding earth events.

7. Many of our subjects who regressed to their preexistence experienced interactions with animals in the spirit world.

## Life-between-Lifetimes

All subjects who had participated in our preexistence studies volunteered to participate in our life-between-lifetimes studies (TR 52, TR 53, TR 54). As with our subjects' preexistence probes, we made no effort to influence their between-lifetimes probes. Typically, our subjects using EM/RC and the Past-life Corridor felt no reluctance in opening their life-between-lifetimes door at the corridor's end. From there, they viewed only briefly their between lifetime existence as spectators before stepping through the door to become active participants, always it seemed in the company of ministering guides. Following their regression experiences, they concluded without exception that the preexistence realm and the life-between-lifetimes realm are not two separate realms at all, but rather one and the same. Together, they provided the unified setting for our past development in the spirit world.

As in their preexistence, our between-lifetimes subjects experienced a collective oneness with all souls while retaining their personal cosmic identity. Also, upon their return to the spirit world, they experienced unconditional love for all souls as in their preexistence. They remained convinced that unconditional love is the supreme force that sustains both physical and spiritual realities.

Our subjects found that preexistence souls and souls with past lifetimes exist together in a spirit realm of indescribable beauty. They interacted freely with ministering teachers, guides and other growth specialists who were always available to promote their evolvement. Without exception, our subjects concluded that in whatever our state—preincarnate, incarnate, or between lifetimes—our evolvement as souls is a forever on-going spiritual phenomenon.

Without exception, our subjects discovered important between-lifetimes experiences with relevance to their present lifetime. Many of them felt that through the regression experience, they had been reunited with important spirit guides from out of their past who would, by invitation, remain with them. When discovered in the company of their spirit guides, any past discarnate experience was found to be relevant. But as with their past lifetimes, their most recent discarnate experiences seem to hold special relevance to their present lifetime.

As in their preexistence, our subjects found that a host of helpers were always available to guide and facilitate their growth during their between-lifetimes intervals. They were able to retrieve whatever was presently relevant to them with the help of their spirit guides. They believed they were guided into the experiences that were important to their continued growth and self-fulfillment.

Our subjects during their between-lifetimes regression often interacted with other discarnates they had known during their past lifetimes, particularly their most recent past lifetime. During their regressed discarnate state, they could assume the gender and personality characteristics of their most recent past lifetime, or for that matter, of any previous lifetime. They interacted with discarnate family members, friends, and even business associates. Their interactions with other discarnates and preincarnates alike were consistently positive and productive.

To experience the afterlife that followed a particular lifetime, our subjects first regressed to that past lifetime after which they opened the between-lifetimes door. In one instance, the regression subject, a twenty-two-year-old graduate student, interacted in the presence of ministering guides with the man who had taken his life in his most recent past lifetime. As it turned out, the victim had himself been a murderer in a previous lifetime, and the murderer had been a past victim. The vicious cycle of "victim to murderer to victim again" had been revealed and finally resolved in the afterlife realm.

In another instance, a student, age twenty, discovered that she had been a suicide victim in her most recent past lifetime. In the afterlife realm, she had been guided by spirit helpers into "soul-embracement," a growth process in which she experienced, rather then censure and punishment, genuine love and acceptance by spiritual helpers. The between-life experiences resulted in a deeper acceptance and understanding of herself as a soul of dignity and worth.

For yet another subject, a nineteen-year-old prelaw major, who had died in infancy in a previous lifetime, had been assisted by spirit helpers to promptly return to earth for another lifetime. Our subjects who had died early in a previous lifetime, however, rejected the concept of "untimely death," even when it involved infancy. They concluded that our transition to afterlife is always timely, purposeful, and growth-related. Over and over again, the disappointments, sufferings, and seemingly tragic deaths were recognized and resolved in the between-life realm. All the resources required were readily available for all who entered that realm.

Our regression studies consistently showed flexibility to be a common thread in all spirit world functions. Highly rigid, intractable procedures were seen as ineffective and counterproductive because they rejected the autonomy of the individual. Spiritual methods used in promoting discarnate growth and preparing souls for a new lifetime recognized the broad spectrum of individual differences and needs.

In our embodied state, our existence could be described as a polarity phenomenon in which we function somewhere between opposites—happiness versus sadness, hope versus despair, independence versus dependence, meaning versus meaninglessness, love versus hate, and good versus evil, to list but a few. Once we become trapped or entangled between poles, our growth can become interrupted, our evolvement can be delayed, and in some cases, our lives can spin out of control. According to our studies, the polarity phenomenon is supplanted by positive re-engagement of the upward growth spiral at the moment of our transition to the other side. Downward, disempowering spirals are reversed to become upward spirals of continued growth. Any lost mental faculty—memory, perception, reasoning, and so forth—is instantly restored at the soul's transition to the other side, with souls resuming their past peaks of growth, a phenomenon we call the *preservation of peak growth* (TR 66).

Our regression studies consistently showed that each afterlife interval integrates the experiences of our most recent past lifetime into a growth pattern that maximizes our past lifetime experiences and prepares us for the next lifetime, should we choose to reincarnate. Following each lifetime, the growth process includes the integration of experiences that may have come beyond our developmental peak for that lifetime. Experiences beyond that peak are resolved in ways that promote our growth in future lifetimes.

For some, the developmental peak for a given lifetime can come at a very early age; for others it can occur very late in adulthood. For souls that squander their potential and waste their growth opportunities, personal growth can reach its peak in the early years. For souls committed to their own development and the good of others, personal growth may reach its very highest level only at their transition to the other side.

In preexistence and between-lifetimes alike, the focus is consistently on the perfection and potentials of souls rather than on faults and limitations. Fortunately, we do not have to wait until our transition to take command of our growth destiny. As souls, we are at present autonomous. We can initiate new growth processes, activate dormant powers, reverse downward spirals, and in the process, discover new meaning to our lives. As we develop our higher potentials, we move beyond a fixated state of existence between poles to a dynamic evolvement of the spirit. We take responsibility for our actions and integrate our life experiences in ways that maximize our own growth potentials while contributing to the growth of others.

As in their preexistence, our between-lifetimes regression subjects found no place for any form of evil on the other side. The mantra, "I will fear no evil," has particular relevance to the spirit realm. Evil is best defined as that which interrupts or impedes our own evolvement or that of others. Evil is by nature self-destructive. Wherever it exists, it consumes itself. No evil accompanies our birth and no evil survives our death. We brought no evil with us when we were born into the world, and we will take no evil with us when we leave it. To attribute evil in any way to the afterlife realm is contradictory to the very nature of that dimension.

Not one of our scores of subjects entering the Past-life Corridor found room for negativity or punishment in either their preexistence or life-between-lifetimes. Although the upward growth spiral ranged from a low level of minimal growth to a high level of abundant growth, they found no downward negative spirals in the spirit world.

Perhaps not surprisingly, there was consensus among our subjects that the growth experiences we accumulate in a lifetime are never lost—they are the rewards of life on this planet. They become the important resources for our continued development in afterlife. They are integrated into our spiritual spiral, where they motivate us to set higher goals and reach higher levels of growth.

Throughout our studies, we found that the interests and activities of our subjects during their present lifetime often seemed to relate to their regression experience. For instance, several of our regression subjects were accomplished musicians. Without exception, they experienced the sounds of music during their regression experience. Some of them spoke of discarnate music as spiritual therapy. Similarly, our subjects who described themselves as animal lovers almost always experienced interactions with animal spirits that were to them spiritually enriching.

Consistent with the views of our subjects who regressed to their preexistence, our between-lifetimes regression subjects concluded that embarking on a future lifetime is a decision made only by the individual, but always with (not under) the guidance and assistance of spiritual helpers and developmental specialists. Loving orientation and generous support in forming goals were typical components of the preparation process.

Though counter to some views, souls in afterlife were never condemned or censured for a previous lifetime. They were never "sentenced" to a particular future lifetime nor prevented from returning to earth for another lifetime. The initiation of a new lifetime was found to be one of the most important decisions souls make. Because the final decision to embark on a new lifetime is made only by the individual, we alone are responsible for our lives and the consequences of our actions. *We do indeed choose to be born.*

Our between-lifetimes regression subjects unanimously concluded that future lifetime events, while often predictable, are not predestined. But although we determine our own destiny as souls, a certain cosmic justice does seem to prevail. For instance, a given extremity in one lifetime is often followed by its opposite in another lifetime. A lifetime of wealth and affluence is often followed by a lifetime of impoverishment and deprivation. Similarly, a lifetime of exploitation of others is often followed by a lifetime of victimization. Such reversals in lifetimes could be explained by the cosmic principle of balance in which two extremes occurring in succession tend to moderate each other to induce a state of balance.

## Past-life Regression and ESP

Throughout our past-life studies, a standard feature of our research was to study our subjects' backgrounds and assess their psychic abilities using standard ESP cards (TR 71). The decision to include psychic assessment in our studies was based on the possibility that insight into our past life could influence our present psychic functions. Our studies confirmed that possibility. With repeated past-life regression, the performance of our subjects on controlled ESP tests for telepathy, clairvoyance, and precognition markedly increased. (As typically defined, telepathy is mind-to-mind communication, clairvoyance is the psychic awareness of existing but unseen realities, and precognition is the psychic awareness of future events.) Regression to preexistence particularly resulted in a dramatic increase in psychic performance in the laboratory. Given insight into their preexistence, several of our subjects demonstrated remarkable mediumistic and channeling powers which they attributed to the attuning and balancing effects of their regression experiences.

Based on these promising findings, we supplemented our past-life regression studies with strategies that targeted in on our subjects' psychic development. Our previous studies had shown that controlled practice increased performance on ESP tests for telepathy, clairvoyance, and precognition. It seemed plausible then, that a controlled strategy in which subjects during hypnosis exercised their psychic abilities could appreciably accelerate their overall psychic development.

To that end, we developed a strategy known as Doors specifically designed to stimulate extrasensory perception (TR 72). The procedure, which has been modified over the years, is still used in our labs and classrooms. It is one of the most powerful procedures known for activating specific psychic functions while promoting the development of our full psychic potential.

The procedure uses self-hypnosis to access certain doors as categories of psychic information. It's important to become familiar with the full procedure before you begin the induction process. Here's the procedure which requires approximately thirty minutes.

## Doors

Find a comfortably safe, quiet place and induce a successful trance state using either the EM/RC procedure or any other preferred strategy. For this application of EM/RC, the procedure is used only to induce a trance state—regression to either childhood or past life is not included.

In the early stages of the procedure, affirm your ability to access your inner sources of psychic information. You can, if you prefer, invoke the protective presence of a spirit guide to accompany you throughout the experience.

Once you have reached a successful trance state, envision yourself entering a long, bright corridor with doors on each side. The doors can be of any shape, color, or material. They can be of wood, gold, silver, glass, or jade, to list but a few of the possibilities. Notice a word inscribed on each door, with the exception of one door which remains blank. The inscription can signify a particular personal interest, such as relationships, career, finances, family, health, and so forth, or it can specify such topics as global events, political issues, or natural catastrophes. The single non-inscribed door is used to gain information regarding any non-specified but relevant topic. You may notice some doors with deeply personal inscriptions such as the name of a certain person or a particular situation. You will notice the doors vary in brightness, with some doors so bright that they command your attention, an indication that they hold special relevance for you at the moment.

As you view the corridor of doors, affirm your ability to open the door of your choice to experience the information it holds for you.

You are now ready to open the door. You can choose to view the unfolding scene or events from the doorway, or you can actually step inside the door to become an active participant, perhaps to alter or in some way influence the activities, particularly when they seem to be precognitive in nature.

During your visit to the corridor, you may choose to open a second door. Opening more than two doors during a single excursion, however, could result in a deluge of information that becomes difficult to accommodate.

To end your visit to the corridor, close the door(s) and briefly contemplate the relevance of the experience. You are now ready to end the trance state by counting from one to five, interspersing suggestions of alertness and well-being.

Once you've returned to the normal state of awareness, reflect on the experience and its relevance. Give special attention to the possible precognitive or clairvoyant content of the experience.

Here are a few examples of the use of this procedure by our subjects:

- During his run for an important office, a political candidate, who was considerably behind in the polls, used Doors in an effort to energize his campaign. Once inside the corridor, he opened a bright gold door with the inscription, CAMPAIGN. Upon opening the door, he discovered that he would win his bid for office, but only if he changed his campaign strategy to emphasize a social issue he had totally overlooked. He modified his campaign accordingly and won the election in a landslide.

• A college student used Doors to discover her future husband. Upon entering the corridor, she was attracted to a bright red, heart-shaped door inscribed with the word, LOVE. She opened the door, whereupon the image of an attractive young man with an engaging smile appeared before her, glowing in a radiance she described as "simply breathtaking." A few days later, she attended a conference where she met the love of her life. He was identical to the image she had seen behind the heart-shaped door.

• An art student used Doors to generate ideas for his artistic creations which included both painting and sculpting. Behind the door inscribed with NEW ART, he saw pictorial representations which literally changed the style and direction of his work. In a later exhibit, his work attracted the attention of critics who praised the artist for his courage to "break away from the sameness of the past."

• An undergraduate student used Doors to identify the graduate program she would later enter. Upon opening the door labeled GRADUATE, a panoramic view of a familiar university stretched out before her. She enrolled in the university's graduate program and upon completing her doctorate, joined the school's faculty.

These are only a few of the possible applications of this interesting strategy.

## *Summary*

Our preexistence and life-between-lifetimes are growth stages that together make up our past development in the spirit world. Rather than two separate dimensions, they are one and the same.

Through EM/RC and Past-life Corridor, we can re-experience our past existence in the spirit realm. The experiences of our past, once integrated into the soul, add meaning and direction to our lives. They provide a strong foundation for our future evolution.

Our past experiences in the spirit realm were consistently empowering. Our growth was nurtured as we nurtured the growth of others. We accessed the wondrous resources available to us in that realm—shimmering pools, sparkling fountains, luminous planes, ministering guides, teachers, and growth specialists.

Fortunately, all the resources of the spirit realm are available to us at the moment. The spirit realm is a spiritual reality. We can tap into it right now to experience it in all its beauty and wonder.

*The eternal mystery of the world is its comprehensibility.*
—ALBERT EINSTEIN (1936)

# THE SPIRIT REALM:
# A PRESENT REALITY

In the two previous chapters, we focused on our past-life experiences with emphasis on their present-life relevance. We examined our existence in past lifetimes and the importance of past-lifetime experiences to our present growth and development. We examined our existence before our first embodiment on earth in that dimension we call our preexistence, with emphasis on the rich resources available to us prior to our first embodiment. Finally, we examined our life-between-lifetimes existence, a disembodied state in a dimension not unlike our preexistence.

We will now focus on the spirit realm as it exists at the moment. We will explore ways we can directly interact with the spirit realm and ways that realm interacts with us.

Our past-life regression studies consistently concluded that the afterlife is a rich continuation of our evolution as souls in a dimension that, like the soul, stretches from everlasting to everlasting. What-ever our state of being, the spirit realm is a place of wondrous growth and spiritual actualization for all souls. It existed for us as a place for growth in the past, and it will exist for us as a place for growth in the future.

Fortunately, we can experience the spirit world as it exists right now. Rather than a far-away place that's our future destination, the spirit realm is a present reality that invites our present interaction. Its closeness is felt more strongly at times, but it is forever present with unlimited enrichment and growth resources. It's a dimension which includes preincarnate as well as discarnate souls, ministering guides, spirit counselors, growth specialists, and other spirit beings, including animals. It consists of many wondrous planes and struc-tures of indescribable beauty and differential growth possibilities.

While that innermost part of our being with its wealth of po-tentials invites our inner probes, the spacious spirit realm with its abundant resources beckons our outer probes. That realm, like our personal existence, is interactive—it does not exist in a vacuum of mystery and isolation. It knocks at the soul's door, inviting interac-tion and enlightenment. It is the immeasurable collective force that under girds, permeates, and sustains all that exists, whether physi-cal or non-physical. You along with all souls are an integral part of it. Wherever you are in your personal growth, you are an evolving soul among all souls.

## Spiritual Interventions

As nature would have it, physical reality alone can be a gateway to spiritual enlightenment. The physical universe at large reflects on a grand scale the endlessness magnificence of the spirit realm. But even a small sliver of the natural world can touch the soul and at-tune us to all that exists. A beautiful sunset, a summer rainstorm, a primeval forest, or a tranquil meadow, for instance, can energize and inspire us to reach new levels of growth.

On a different but equally important scale, nature's quiet harbingers can be channels for comforting messages and healing energies from the other side. For a former student whose father had recently crossed to the other side, the messenger was a colorful butterfly. Here's her account:

> The shimmering water of the pool reflected the sun and summer blue of the sky. It reminded me of my childhood near the sea and my seafaring father. Now I was a dorm resident and the nearest body of water was a swimming pool.
>
> As I sat beside the pool, I felt the weight of grief over the sudden loss of my father, and the guilt of having not been there to comfort him at his crossing. Suddenly, a colorful orange and black butterfly descended and lit upon my hand. I marveled at its gossamer weight and stillness. I thought of my father, how he had loved the sea and the out-of-doors. He believed in the healing energies of nature and the eternal power of oneness with the universe.
>
> Momentarily, the butterfly took flight, and I felt an almost imperceptible tug as though a gossamer thread had been broken. Simultaneously, I sensed a release of guilt and grief, and a wondrous awareness of my father's loving presence.

In addition to the comfort and healing they often provide, interventions from the spirit realm can involve very practical, everyday concerns as well as crisis situations. They have been known to warn of impending danger, offer guidance in decision making, and provide solutions to critical problems. They can be either direct or indirect manifestations of the caring, compassionate nature of that dimension.

What may have been a very direct intervention from the other side occurred in my life several years ago at a time of family crisis. I was an undergraduate student at the University of Alabama when I received an emergency call to return home because of a serious injury my brother had sustained in a motorcycle accident. Although I had no transportation of my own and insufficient funds for the trip, I dressed for travel in my only suit, a high school graduation gift which I had already begun to associate with good fortune. I had found that wearing the suit on final exams seemed somehow to improve my test performance. Even if it were a mental thing, I credited the suit with helping it along.

Dressed in the blue suit, I reached into the pocket and found to my utter amazement a new, neatly folded one-hundred dollar bill, more than sufficient for the round-trip ticket home. As it turned out, my brother's injuries were not as serious as first thought so I returned to campus the next day.

To this day, I have no clear explanation for the money's appearance in my suit pocket. Could it have been a benevolent intervention of the spirit world? Is the materialization of tangible objects, even money, beyond the powers of the other side? We now know that the spirit realm stands poised with abundant power to enrich our lives, often unexpectedly and upon very short notice. It happens to us all, even in ways that may never come to our attention.

Comforting interventions from the other side seem often to occur at times of serious illness. For a student whose mother was near death in comatose state, the intervention happened just hours before her mother's transition. By her report, she was sitting with her hospitalized mother when a glowing figure of a young man appeared at her mother's bedside around midnight. The radiant figure, dressed in a flowing garment and wearing a turban, stood at the bedside for several moments before slowly fading away when a nurse entered the room.

Near dawn, her mother awoke from the coma and with a smile, turned to her daughter and asked, "Did you see that wonderful friend who visited me in the night? He was wearing a turban." With that, she closed her eyes and peacefully crossed over. Comforted by the experience, the student accepted the death of her mother with complete assurance that her mother's passage to the other side was a joyous transition in the company of a compassionate, loving guide.

The need for interaction between the departed and those left behind often continues far beyond the soul's transition to the other side. Why should the needs of survivors to relate to souls whose conscious existence continues on the other side be thwarted or denied? Similarly, why should the soul's transition eliminate all possibility of further communication with loved ones and friends left behind, a phenomenon we call discarnate manifestation? Fortunately, the communication channels between these dimensions do remain open.

The interaction with the other side is often initiated by the departed who understand the importance of the interaction. Here's an example.

A former honor student, upon completing his Bachelor of Science degree, assumed an administrative position with a financial institution where he rapidly advanced in the corporate structure. As his instructor and academic advisor, I had been impressed by his excellent academic performance and outstanding leadership skills.

A few years following his graduation, I was awakened in the middle of the night to see his image enveloped in a radiant glow at the foot of my bed. Smiling broadly, he appeared only momentarily before slowly fading into the night. I knew immediately that he had crossed over.

The next morning, I received a call at my office from his mother with details of her son's recent illness and death. His promising career had been interrupted when he was diagnosed with a cancerous tumor. Although the prognosis for his recovery was good, he unfortunately died during surgery.

Still coping with grief over the sudden loss, she recounted how he had twice appeared to her in the night as a brief radiant image, always smiling. She explained that until her son's visits, she believed that any communication between the living and deceased was impossible because of a "great gulf" separating them. Through her son's visits, she had come to understand firsthand that interacting with the departed is a natural healing and empowering process for the departed and survivor alike. Interacting with her son enabled her to accept his death, not as a tragedy, but as a natural transition to another dimension of continued growth and fulfillment.

Experience teaches us all that to reject the possibility of interacting with the departed imposes an unnatural distance between dimensions and unnecessarily thwarts two very basic human needs: (1) our need to communicate with loved ones who precede us to the other side and (2) their need to communicate with us.

## *The Power of Authentic Love*

As discussed previously, many of our regression subjects experienced a condition in their past life which they described as *real love*. Real love was authentic and unconditional. It permeated their preexistence as well as life-between-lifetimes. It should not be surprising then to find that authentic love survives death and connects dimensions. It is often the underlying force that energizes discarnate interactions.

Nothing is more important to our spiritual evolution than authentic love. It is the purest and noblest expression of the human soul. It is through authentic love that we energize our personal growth spiral and promote the spiritual evolution of others. Authentic love, as the song goes, "is greater far than tongue or pen can ever tell. It goes beyond the highest star and reaches to the lowest hell." Authentic love is rich, pure, measureless, and strong. Equally as important, it endures forever.

One of my very earliest studies conducted as a doctoral student at the University of Alabama found authentic love to be a powerful rejuvenating force (TR 2). Even in a love relationship interrupted by death, real love can continue to inspire and empower. Throughout the study designed to uncover the secrets of longevity, a recurrent theme was the rejuvenating effects of an enduring love relationship, even when the love partner was deceased.

The power of real love to span dimensions was dramatically illustrated during my interview with a retired professor of mathematics. Early on in the interview, I noted that she often stroked a large emerald pendant, which she noted was a gift from her deceased husband. She claimed that upon stroking the emerald, she always sensed the loving presence of her husband. The emerald as a symbol of their love, she believed, was a channel that linked her to her husband and enabled her to interact with him. She attributed her excellent health and the rich quality of her life to the power of that interaction.

Supportive of her claim, the emerald was found in that early study to be the number one gem of choice for subjects age 90 and older. It was believed by many of them to possess inherent rejuvenating properties. In contrast to the emerald, the diamond was believed by our subjects to induce fatigue and literally deplete the body of rejuvenating energy. That finding, once circulated, initiated an interesting local trend—that of trading in diamonds for emeralds.

## A Love Story

A much later research study conducted at Athens State University further illustrated the power of love, particularly first love, to survive bodily death (TR 81). That seemed to be the case with Abigail, an actress whose developing first love seemed to explain her reoccurring apparition at Athens State University soon after her death and continuing till this day. Students, alumni, and campus guests alike, including many who were unfamiliar with the legend, have reported seeing the willowy figure keeping her late night vigil, either from a third floor window of McCandless Hall or on the stage where she performed, almost always with a bouquet of red roses clutched at her breast.

As the story goes, Abigail Burns was a rising opera singer from Philadelphia and a friend of the school's president in the early 1900s. On a brief visit to the campus, the beautiful actress met the small town's dashing young attorney, and at first sight they fell in love. It was the first love for both. Each day they met in the art studio on the third floor of McCandless Hall, a stately Greek Revival structure with a large auditorium on the first floor where she would later perform.

On the final evening of her visit, she performed selections from Verdi's opera *La Traviata* to students and specially invited guests in the Hall's auditorium. She was adored by the crowd, and upon receiving an enthusiastic ovation and a bouquet of red roses, she promised, "I will return soon."

Before departing that night for the long carriage ride to her next engagement, as the legend goes, she hurriedly met once again with her newfound love in the third-floor art studio where they pledged anew their undying love for each other. It was there that she promised as before, "I will return soon."

Later that night, her horse-drawn carriage was caught in a dangerous storm with lightning, thunder, and torrents of rain. The driver sought a safe place to stop along the treacherous road, but to no avail. Eventually, they approached a bridge where the horses, frightened by lightning and a burst of thunder, suddenly lunged forward, disengaging the carriage. The driver leapt to safety, but Abigail stayed with the carriage, which lunged over the bridge and crashed onto the bedrock below. Mortally wounded, she was pulled by the driver from the wreckage, still clutching the bouquet of red roses. Her last words were, "I've a promise to keep. I must return."

Shortly after her death, she apparently fulfilled her promise—the radiant image of Abigail with red roses clutched at her breast appeared first at the window of the art studio and then on the stage of McCandless Hall where she had performed. Until this day, the image continues periodically to appear, typically late in the evening hours. It is almost always visible at the art studio window around midnight on November 12, which is said to be the anniversary of her death.

Just to the side of McCandless Hall still stands a large hackberry tree planted shortly after Abigail's death in memory of the actress who was to become a legend known around the world.

*Figure 4. McCandless Hall, Athens State University.*
*The willowy image of Abigail is often seen at a third-floor window, or on the first-floor auditorium stage of this historic building.*

But the story of Abigail does not end with the legend itself. Our research of the legend included an examination of sparse existing records as well as the use of certain hands-on procedures, including a strategy called *Interfacing* (TR 27). Developed in our labs for exploring the afterlife, Interfacing is based on the premise that only a thin veil hangs between physical and spiritual dimensions; consequently they often merge spontaneously to interact with each other. The procedure was designed to deliberately promote that process.

Interfacing, a group procedure, is usually conducted on site where a manifestation of merging has already occurred. The setup for the procedure consists of a table around which is seated a group of volunteer participants, who can be surround by an audience of spectators. Although in some ways similar to the séance, Interfacing does not require the presence of an experienced medium. According to this procedure, the mediumistic potential to some degree is common to everyone. By bringing together physical and spiritual dimensions, the procedure can spontaneously activate the mediumistic potentials of its participants.

To research the legend of Abigail using Interfacing, forty-six college students enrolled in a parapsychology seminar assembled on the stage of McCandless Hall where Abigail performed and where her recurring apparition had been seen. Eight students (five men and three women) volunteered as active participants with the remaining students seated around them.

To initiate merging, participants at the table joined hands in symbolic unity and then affirmed their receptiveness to interacting with the discarnate realm. No effort was made to bring forth Abigail specifically, but rather to make each participant receptive to the merging process and the interaction that usually follows.

Almost instantly, a sense of Abigail's presence settled over the group. Participants at the table then engaged in an intensely moving interaction with Abigail. To members of the group, it was almost as though she were physically present. They communicated with her, and periodically throughout the interaction, they shared with each other their impressions and the specifics of Abigail's messages. Through them, Abigail confirmed the essential elements of the legend, to include her visit to the campus, her relationship with the town's young attorney, and her performance of selections from *La Traviata*. She verified the circumstances of her death and her recurring visits to the art studio spanning almost a century.

As the session progressed, a prelaw student seated at the table entered what seemed to be a trance-mediumship state in which Abigail spoke directly to the group through him. She explained her visitations as a manifestation of love which can, she said, span a lifetime and beyond. Following her death, according to Abigail, the young attorney, like herself, was drawn to the art studio. There they continued to meet long after her death as a testament of their deep love for each other. Her frequent presence in McCandless Hall, she insisted, was not because of an unfilled promise, but "because of love."

Although it was unclear as to what eventually happened to the lover Abigail left behind, the prelaw student made an interesting assertion at the close of the Interface session: It was he in another lifetime who had been Abigail's lover. He was convinced that the Interface session reunited him with Abigail once again. For him, it illustrated the power of love to survive a lifetime and beyond. He concluded, "Real love is forever. It is power in its purest form."

The prelaw student, who is today a practicing attorney, later participated in our past-life regression studies using EM/RC and the Past-life Corridor. His regression experiences confirmed his brief but intense past-life relationship with Abigail. He believes that he will always feel a love connection to her.

## *Authentic Love versus Arrogant Judgment*

The power of authentic love can connect dimensions in many different ways. In some instances, it can be an enlightening interaction that teaches us important lessons about life. My grandfather, whose great love for animals I mentioned earlier, recognized the power of authentic love which he often illustrated through stories from out of his past. One story in particular stands out above all the rest as a manifestation of not only the power of authentic love but also the consequences of arrogant condemnation of others.

It was a weekend like many others when my brothers and I visited our grandparents, often staying over and listening to stories late into the night around a roaring fireplace. You will perhaps recall my previous account of one such visit on a stormy night after my grandmother had transported us in her surrey over a swollen stream. On this particular night, a northwestern front had moved through and instead of rain, it had begun to snow.

As we gathered around the fireplace, my grandfather began a story I would always remember about his childhood in a small Tennessee town in the 1800s. In his small world, everyone knew of a notorious outlaw who had grown up in the same town. Rumor had it that the outlaw had killed scores of men and robbed several banks throughout southern Tennessee before continuing his crime spree across Arkansas, Oklahoma, and into the panhandle of Texas. Finally, the town received word that the young outlaw had been shot dead, reportedly by the brother of a man he had himself killed.

Soon, his body was returned for burial to his small hometown. Rather than a church funeral, a simple graveside ceremony was arranged. It was on a dreary winter afternoon when the casket carried by six men was brought to the country graveyard for burial in a hand-dug grave of at least six feet deep, which was customary for those days.

Despite freezing rain, the townspeople, including my grandfather, who was then around five, gathered en masse with umbrellas at the graveside for the funeral of the notorious outlaw. With the bandit's grieving mother seated at the graveside, the tall, lean preacher took his customary place at the head of the casket, his Bible in hand ready to direct the interment. Three men standing on each side of the grave gripped in their hands large ropes that went under the casket to support it and later to lower it into the open grave. It was by then nearing dark, and the ropes and casket alike had become coated with ice from the freezing rain.

As the preacher and townspeople looked on, the pallbearers with ropes in hand suddenly lost their grip. The ice-coated ropes slipped through their hands, and the casket plummeted topside down into the deep grave, splashing into water that had begun to seep in. An eerie silence fell over the group while the preacher from his position at the head of the grave kept his face frozen in a solemn look. To abruptly conclude the ceremony, if you could call it that, the preacher arrogantly bit out, "The outlaw just fell into hell!" The grieving mother was then led away, and with the casket remaining topside down, men with shovels filled the grave.

"But the story does not end there," my grandfather was quick to add. That night, the preacher was suddenly awakened from sleep around midnight by the shining specter of the outlaw standing at the foot of his bed. With his piercing eyes fixed on the alarmed preacher, he said with cold calculation, "I ain't in hell yet!" With that, the outlaw, his fiery eyes still fixed on the preacher, slowly vanished. The frightened preacher tossed restlessly for the remainder of the night.

"But," my grandfather again added, "the story does not end there." The next night, at around midnight, the luminous image of the outlaw again appeared at the foot of the preacher's bed with the same message, "I ain't in hell yet!" before slowly fading into the darkness. And again on the third night, the outlaw appeared exactly as before with the same message.

When morning broke on the third day, the preacher, exhausted from lack of sleep, called a special meeting of the townspeople to consider, according to him, "a most urgent matter." At the appointed time, the hollow-eyed preacher, his voice no longer laced with arrogance, addressed the overflowing crowd assembled in the small village church with the simple message, "Judge not that ye be not judged. In disrespectful arrogance and condemnation, I judged a man I called an outlaw, and that judgment came back three nights in a row to haunt me." He then offered a remorseful apology, not only to the people gathered, but to the man he had judged as well. He concluded the meeting with the words, "Let us love one another."

Never again did the apparition appear to disturb the preacher's sleep, and never again did the preacher judge another in reckless arrogance.

My grandfather always ended his stories with the question, "So what do you think of that?" Instead of moralizing, he left it to us to draw our own conclusions.

## The Power of Humor

Humor, like love, has a power all its own. In my studies of longevity, a sense of humor was found to be so critical to a long, quality life that I called it the Holy Grail of rejuvenation (TR 41).

The power of humor to span dimensions and connect us to the other side is impressively illustrated by another series of well-known manifestations of afterlife at Athens State University. Over the years, the manifestations gave rise to the legend of Bart, a stable boy in the mid-1800s at the school then known as Athens Female Academy, a private school for women founded in 1822.

According to the legend, Bart tended the horses for the school's president, Madame Childs, and occasionally was her surrey driver. Very attractive and muscular in build, he was young and playful, but according to some, mentally underdeveloped.

At the school's social events, typically held in the spacious parlor of Founders Hall, the stable boy would often help with serving or when not serving stand formally dressed near the school's president, ready to assist her if called upon. His sense of humor and natural good looks seemed always to light up the party.

*Figure 5. Founders Hall, Athens State University.*
*The stable boy is often seen in the parlor or second-floor chapel*
*of this magnificent building.*

When not participating in the school's festive activities, he often observed them from a distance. To the delight of students, he would sometimes be seen playfully peeping from behind a curtain or around a door. He was known occasionally to play tricks on the students, mischievously hiding a piece of jewelry and other personal item. According to one report, he once hid a lady's glove in a vase on the parlor's mantle, only to discover it himself after a long, exhaustive search by the students. For that, he was awarded a light kiss. Afterward, the vase became a favorite hiding place for the little personal items he purloined from the students.

Adored by the young women, he was known to appear occasionally with his sleeves rolled up high to reveal his tanned, muscular arms, or with his shirt opened half-way to his waist to display well-developed abs. His smile was pure male beauty. Although he seemed to thrive on the attention of students, he never strayed beyond the bounds of his position as stable boy.

Unfortunately, tragedy would soon befall the stable boy. According to reports, while working in the stables he was kicked by a horse and sustained a fatal head injury. His funeral, which was conducted in the school's chapel on the second floor of Founders Hall, was a stately, elaborate affair with anthems, psalms, and glowing tributes from students and Madame Childs. The interment in a graveyard adjacent to the school was likewise stately, with flower petals scattered on the coffin as it was gently lowered into the grave.

A period of mourning followed for the beloved stable boy, who had by then been elevated almost to sainthood. But an interesting turn of events was soon to follow. First were the subtle stirring of parlor curtains, followed by the unexplained turning out of lamps, and finally the appearance of his shadowy image in the dim hallways of Founders Hall. Once the school's social events resumed, the stable boy would often appear, peeking as before from behind a curtain or around a door and flashing a broad smile.

Soon, the young women's personal items began to disappear as before, only to reappear in the most unlikely places. For instance, a missing umbrella showed up hanging mysteriously from a high curtain rod, and a lady's fan was found half concealed in a crystal chandelier. Finally, a misplaced glove showed up in the stable boy's favorite hiding place—the old Paris vase on the parlor's mantel. That telltale clue signaled to the delight of all the return of the stable boy; and best of all, he was his old self again.

*Figure 6. Old Paris Vase.*
*In this old vase, Bart hid items playfully taken from students.*

Our research, which included interviews with witnesses as well as an examination of existing records, found considerable evidence supporting the legend of Bart (TR 28). The school had stables that housed Madame Childs' horses in the mid-1800s, and she frequently traveled by carriage with a young stable boy as her driver. True to the legend, the stable boy, whose name was Bartholomew, died in the stables after being kicked by a horse. Shortly after his death, his apparition was seen by students as well as Madame Childs in the parlor and hallways of Founders Hall.

As an interesting aside, legend has it that following Bart's death, condolences were sent to Madame Childs from President Lincoln who was known to be her personal friend and who had earlier intervened during the Battle of Athens to save Founders Hall from being burned by Federal troops.

To this day, Bart still haunts—or perhaps better put, frequents —the parlor and hallways of Founders Hall. The harmless manifestations seem obviously designed not to frighten or in any way intimidate, but rather to simply socialize or charm.

In a recent amusing encounter with the stable boy, two women students who were enrolled in my course returned late at night to their dormitory room on the third floor of Founders Hall to find a shaft of very bright light falling suspiciously into the hallway from under the room's door. They cautiously opened the door, only to find the light came not from the room itself but from under the room's closet door. With apprehension, they opened the closet door to find standing before them the gleaming image of a young, attractive male, very muscular in build and smiling mischievously. Adding to their not necessarily unpleasant surprise, he was totally nude! Still smiling broadly, he slowly faded, leaving the room in darkness.

The legend of Bart, its essential elements for the most part verified, is important to our study of the afterlife for several reasons. First and foremost, it seems to confirm with clarity the continuation of individual identity and personality beyond death. Furthermore, it suggests that there is an important place for humor in the afterlife. It shows that a healthy sense of humor, like real love, is a powerful force that can enrich the quality of our existence, not only in this lifetime, but in the hereafter as well.

A healthy sense of humor can literally break Karmic bands and clear Karmic debts. It helps us to bring ourselves into balance and find that place of joy within. It rejuvenates and promotes good health—mentally, physically, and spiritually. It releases resentment, anger, and other negative expressions that limit our growth. When we view disappointments and adversity through the prism of optimism and humor, we clear out negativity and reach into the spiritual realm. We break all limiting bands and extend the boundaries for our growth. We find our way out of the prisons we too often build for ourselves.

## *Animals in Afterlife*

My early love for animals had its beginning with my parents and grandparents alike who always treated animals as beings of great worth. As a child growing up on a southern farm, I often observed my mother compassionately caressing sick or injured animals, calling them by name, and talking gently to them. Though she never mentioned it, she obviously connected with them mentally in ways that promoted their recovery. Her gentle manner alone seemed to bring comfort and healing. Until her recent death at age ninety-six, she never turned away a stray animal that showed up at her door.

Like my mother, my father always showed a deep respect and love for animals. In caring for farm animals, he often performed what seemed to be a comforting aura massage in which he gently stroked the external energies of an ill or injured animal, a technique we today call the aura massage. It was through my father, in fact, that I learned to see the aura of animals. I had always spontaneously seen the auras around persons, and I assumed that everyone else saw them as well, though I did not know to call them auras. I remember often seeing my father at a great distance and always recognizing him because of his expansive aura, a radiant blue like the color of his eyes. In viewing animal auras, my father suggested that simply looking beyond the animal was sufficient to bring the aura into full view. I tried, and it worked!

From my earliest childhood, animals as friends have enriched my life and taught me many important lessons—trust, loyalty, courage, and affection, to list but a few. By interacting with animals and nurturing them, not as their owners, but as their friends, protectors, and caregivers, we learn to value them as beings worthy of our love and respect. They can bring comfort, companionship, and joy into our lives. As friends, they often meet our needs for playfulness, relaxation, and acceptance.

I have never doubted the spiritual nature of animals. When it comes time for animals to cross over, once they have become a part of your life, it is consoling to know that life continues for them, as it does for us, on the other side. That awareness was especially comforting to my three children at a time of great loss when their longtime playmate, a beautiful white dog of mixed breed, crossed over.

Whitey, as he was called, had been their companion for several years. When school was in session, he would see them off by bus and then wait patiently with amazing timing for their return at the end of the lane leading up to our house. During summer vacations on the farm, he would romp with them in the open fields, swim with them in the pond, and join them in his favorite game—playing ball.

It was a lazy summer afternoon when tragedy struck. The children were playing in the lane when Whitey ventured onto the road and was struck by an oncoming car. The driver, a young man I guessed to be in his twenties, stopped and carefully retrieved the fatally injured dog. He brought the unconscious dog up the lane in his arms and gently placed him on the ground. As we all knelt around our dying friend, my older brother looked up through his tears at the stranger, who was also weeping, and said, "It'll be okay. Dogs go to heaven when they die."

Whitey died and we buried him on the farm in a special place we had set aside years earlier for our animal friends that crossed over. Although we would never see the young stranger again, we would never forget the compassion and deep understanding he showed at our time of loss.

Many years later, I was reminded of Whitey during a study I was leading at Athens State University on survival of bodily death. A professor of physics at another university who had heard of our research called my office early one morning with the question, "Do dogs have an afterlife?" Before I could answer, she explained that her dog, Dax, had recently died unexpectedly. She and her husband were devastated by the sudden death of the beloved animal that had been the joy of their lives for many years. Each night, they would step onto the balcony of their upstairs bedroom to say good-night to Dax. He would always respond with excitement—running, barking, and leaping excitedly among the shrubs.

They had no children, and with Dax gone, it was as though a part of their lives went with him. Then, on the night before her call, a remarkable thing happened. According to her account, she and her husband had just returned home from dinner and were in their upstairs bedroom preparing to retire. "Zombie-like," she said, "I stepped out onto the balcony for the first time since Dax's death." From there, to her amazement, she saw Dax below—playing, running, leaping about with obvious joy. He glistened in the bright moonlight as silvery beams seemed to bounce off him in a stunning display of light.

In wonderment but without mentioning Dax, she called to her husband and calmly asked him to join her on the balcony where he too saw Dax. Embracing each other, they watched Dax running about with incredible joy until finally he leaped upward and disappeared. Instantly, their grief lifted. The pain of their loss had been replaced by the wonder of Dax's appearance and the awareness of his continued existence in another world.

She concluded her call with the words: "Well, I guess I've answered my own question—Dogs do have an afterlife!" I added: "Not only do they have an afterlife, they often want us to know about it and share in their joy."

In a later call to my office, she recalled the experience as a valuable turning point for her and her husband. She explained, "It instantly changed our views of life and death."

For many of us, the existence of animals in afterlife makes the other side a far more attractive and appealing place.

## *Embracing the Other Side*

As previously discussed, very important interactions with the other side often occur during Interfacing, a group procedure in which our dimension of reality merges and interacts with the other side. By way of review, the procedure is in some ways similar to the séance, but it does not require the presence of an experienced medium. The merging of dimensions can spontaneously activate the mediumistic potentials of any of its participants.

In a very productive Interfacing session conducted recently in our laboratory, a college student interacted with her deceased father to gain important practical information related to her present life situation (TR 81). The setup for the session consisted of a table around which were seated six participants, including the student, and a surrounding audience of twenty observers. Although the participants had no previous experience with Interfacing, they had been oriented concerning the procedure and were receptive to the concept.

Early in the session, several entities interacted with the group before the student's deceased father came forth and began communicating directly with her. It was her first interaction with her father since his death in an auto accident two years earlier. After a very touching exchange between father and daughter, silence fell over the group during which the student seemed to still be in touch with her father for several minutes before the interaction finally ended.

The Interfacing experience with her father was a very poignant moment for the student. At a visit to my office the next day, she described the interaction as so realistic that it was as if her father were actually present. Mentally, she had seen him and actually heard his voice. By her report, he instructed her during the interval of silence to search through a box of magazines still stored in his home office. She searched through the magazines to find hidden among their pages a large sum of money he had squirreled away to cover her college expenses.

## The Apparition at the Window

As I earlier noted, the discarnate realm often knocks at our door to initiate the interaction from that side, always with a purpose. It seems that our loved ones who precede us to the other side carry with them not only their need to communicate, but their interests and concerns for our well-being as well. As already illustrated, that concern can include even monetary matters. I remember a very highly successful merchant and friend of my parents who died suddenly of a massive heart attack. It was soon after the Great Depression during which many banks had failed, including his own local bank. In those days of bank failures and financial losses, confidence in financial institutions was at an all-time low. It became a common practice to either store money or bury it in a secure place rather than to entrust it with banks.

Soon after the merchant's death, his family made an exhaustive search for what they believed to be a large sum of missing funds. They searched throughout the residence, including closets, storage spaces, and the attic. They searched the surrounding premises, including a wash house, stables, and vacant servants' quarters. They even searched what they thought could be possible burying places, all without success. They failed to search, however, an old storage building located at a considerable distance from the residence.

A few months after his death, the merchant's full image was seen by a family member late at night in the upstairs window of the old storage building. Standing at the window as if beckoning attention, the recurring apparition was soon to be seen by other family members and strangers alike.

Finally, the merchant's son decided to search the old building. Among the discarded items scattered about in the upstairs room, he noticed in a corner a very large metal trunk. He pried the trunk open to find it filled with the missing money. The old building in its remote location was probably seen by the merchant as a safe hiding place in case of fire at the main residence. With the money finally recovered, the apparition of the merchant at the window promptly ceased, never to appear again.

## Healing Orb of Energy

Discarnate manifestations do not always occur in human form. Orbs and points of light are among the most commonly observed phenomena. They can occur almost anywhere. They often appear as recurring manifestations in a variety of settings believed to be haunted, or they can emerge spontaneously during such structured procedures as Interfacing and table tipping.

A psychologist whose father had recently died observed a point of light which she described as a star moving slowly about the ceiling of her bedroom during the night. Accompanying the manifestation was an unmistakable sense of her father's presence. Comforted by the experience, she thanked her father and the point of light gently faded.

A green iridescent orb was seen for many years in Brown Hall on the campus of Athens State University. Typically observed in a window over the building's front balcony, the orb was believed to be associated with the building's history as an infirmary in the early 1900s.

The orb's iridescent green suggested probable healing properties. To investigate that possibility, a group of students enrolled in my class in Experimental Parapsychology arranged an Interfacing session in the room where the sphere was typically sighted (TR 55). With the group gathered at night around a small table, the radiant green orb appeared at the center of the room, first near the ceiling and then slowly descending to hover directly over the table where it remained for the duration of the session.

As stillness fell over the group, a pre-med student who had recently sustained a wrist injury boldly reached her swollen arm into the orb and instantly experienced complete relief of pain. By the end of the two-hour session, the swelling was totally gone.

Following discovery of the orb's healing powers, I began using it regularly with my patients to alleviate pain and accelerate healing. As word of the orb's healing properties spread, the pre-med student who had been so impressed with the amazing healing energy of the orb returned to campus as a practicing physician to inquire about the possibility of using the orb for her patients. Unfortunately, by then the orb had vanished. Following the extensive renovation of the building, the orb that had been observed for almost a century disappeared forever.

*Figure 7. Brown Hall, Athens State University.*
*For almost a century, a green orb of energy was seen*
*in a window over the building's front balcony.*

## Table Tipping

Table tipping, sometimes called tabling, has become increasingly popular in recent years as a highly productive strategy for interacting with the spirit world. It was first observed in nineteenth century séances in which the table tilted or levitated and then tapped on the ground certain coded messages from the spirit world. With a medium present, the tipping usually occurred after contact with a particular entity had been established. Although table tipping as practiced today does not require a medium, participants at the table can experience mediumistic interactions in which they become messengers for a discarnate presence.

Table tipping requires a quiet setting free of distractions with a small group of participants seated comfortably around a small table such as a card table. The setting can also include an observing audience that is typically seated in a circular arrangement around the participants. The session is usually initiated with a strategy called "opening the table" in which the participants join hands as a symbol of oneness and then formulate their objectives.

Typically, the overall objective in table tipping is to communicate with discarnate entities but without any effort to invoke or "call up" a particular entity. More specific objectives can include developing one's skills at tabling, increasing one's understanding of the afterlife, and acquiring information of a personal nature, to list but a few of the possibilities. After objectives have been formulated, participants place their hands, palm sides down, lightly upon the table and await any manifestation in the table.

A mild pulsation or vibration in the table typically signals a spirit presence. Participants then work with the table, not against it so as not to influence the table while remaining receptive to it. Once the table tilts and remains in the tilted position, the group verbally acknowledges the responding presence and establishes a communication code, typically one tap of the table on the ground for a "yes" response, two taps for a "no" response, and three taps for either "indecisive or cannot answer" response to the group's questions. Questions can then be addressed to the spirit presence, either from participants at the table, or when present and with permission of the group, an audience observer. Throughout the interaction, the table returns to the tilted position after each response to await other questions. Once the interaction with a particular presence ends, the table returns to its resting state. Participants can then either continue with other interactions or end the session. To end the session, participants express their gratitude for the interaction and then discuss with the full group the results of the session.

In table tipping, information can be received through an extensive range of table movements called table kinesics. Aside from the standard "yes," "no," and "indecisive or cannot answer" responses, table kinesics includes such response patterns as hesitation, repeated or sequential tapping, light or heavy tapping, slow or rapid tapping, and vibrations. A powerful tapping of the table indicates intensity or authority whereas a gentle tapping signals caring and understanding. Strong vibrations in the table which often occur before tilting suggest the presence of a very strong entity with an urgent need to communicate; whereas less intense vibrations or soft pulsations are associated with a reserved presence, possibly one who is communicating through tabling for the first time. Repetitive tapping to a single question suggests either a need to restate the question or interruption from another source.

In rare instances, the table has been known to either totally levitate with all legs clearing the ground, or to tilt on one leg and then spin around in a circle, patterns that suggest a very intense interaction with a strong entity or the collective expression of several entities.

Occasionally during table tipping, a discarnate presence will materialize to be collectively perceived by the total group. This rare phenomenon occurred during a tabling session with college students in the chapel of Founders Hall at Athens State University. During the session, the stable boy from the 1850s who, as discussed earlier, frequented the building following his accidental death, communicated through the table that he was content on the other side, and that his visits to Founders Hall were simply enjoyable diversions. He then appeared before the group as a glowing image, smiling broadly and his eyes sparkling. He was seen clearly by the total group, which consisted of eight students seated at the table (one student on each side and one student at each corner) surrounded by the remaining class of thirty-two students.

Table tipping can be an invaluable source of comfort and reassurance for survivors left behind, particularly in instances of the sudden, unexpected death of a friend or family member. Beyond simply affirming survival of bodily death, tabling can satisfy our need to interact and share our feelings again with the departed. By the same token, it offers them the opportunity to interact directly with us.

Table tipping can involve matters of life and death importance. For me personally, table tipping may have literally saved my life by providing important information concerning a future accident. At that time, I commuted daily to my work in another city. Typically, I took the shorter route, a U.S. highway, but occasionally I traveled by interstate to avoid heavy city traffic. During the table tipping session conducted in my campus office, the source provided the date and other detailed information concerning a serious accident which it predicted would occur on the U.S. highway I normally traveled.

On the designated date, I took the advice of the table and traveled the interstate rather than the U.S. highway. I discovered later in the day that a serious accident involving an eighteen-wheeler and several cars had occurred on the U.S. highway exactly as predicted by the table.

Table tipping can be conducted almost anywhere, as long as the setting is quiet and free of distractions as earlier noted. Table tipping has been conducted at the Pentagon, major colleges and universities, churches, community centers, retirement homes, high schools, executive suites of major corporations, and even the White House. Private jets, cruise ships, and trains have also been sites of table tipping. Among my favorite places for table tipping is the shade of a magnificent oak standing alone in a meadow near my house. Other favorite places are the islands of the Caribbean, particularly Grand Cayman.

## *Table Tipping in Moonlight*

There's something about moonlight that adds interest and excitement to almost any activity, especially table tipping. Among my most extraordinary table tipping experiences was a session with college students conducted under a full moon in front of Founders Hall at Athens State University in an open area known as "Founders Green" (TR 49). In the final stage of the session, the table totally levitated with all legs clearing the ground. While total levitation when tabling is rare, it does sometimes occur, typically to accentuate the importance and empowerment possibilities of interacting with the other side.

For the Founders Green session, thirty-eight students enrolled in my course in experimental parapsychology gathered on an early fall evening with a full harvest moon rising on the horizon. With four volunteer participants seated at a card table, the remaining students were either seated on the ground or standing in a circular arrangement. Here's a full transcript of the audio recorded session.

Group:    (with the table in tilted position): Thank you for meeting with us here under the full moon. We welcome the opportunity of interacting with you. Would you agree to answer our questions by giving one tap of the table on the ground for "yes," two taps for "no," and three taps for "indecisive or cannot answer"?

Table:    Yes (indicated by one tap).

Group:    Do you have a message for a specific person in this group?

Table:    No (indicated by two taps).

Group:    Is your message for everyone in this group?

Table:    Yes.

Group:    Does your message to this group concern the afterlife?

Table:    Yes.

Group:    Have you had a lifetime on earth?

Table:    Yes.

Group:    Many lifetimes?

Table:    Yes.

Group:    Did you choose for yourself whether to embark on a new lifetime on earth?

Table:    Yes.

Group:    Is a lifetime ever forced upon anyone?

Table:    No.

Group:    Is this your opinion only?

Table:    No.

Group:    Are there other spirit beings with you right now who are aware of this interaction?

Table:    Yes.

Group:    Are they in full accord with the answers you give us?

Table:    Undecided or cannot answer (indicated by three taps).

Group:    Should they not be in full accord with your answers, could you indicate this by answering first for yourself, and then giving three additional taps?

Table:    Yes.

Group:    Could we refer to the others present as the "council"?

Table:    Yes (following a long hesitation in which the source was apparently consulting others present).

Group:    We get the impression that the others present do not like to be labeled "council," right?

Table:    Yes.

Group:    But for lack of a better word, they approve of our using "council"?

| | |
|---|---|
| Table: | Yes. |
| Group: | Are you yourself a part of that council? |
| Table: | Yes. |
| Group: | We would like to know more about the members of the council. Are they there, like you, to share information? |
| Table: | Yes (following hesitation). |
| Group: | And to interact in other ways as well? |
| Table: | Yes. |
| Group: | Do you represent them? |
| Table: | No. |
| Group: | Are they there because you value their collective wisdom? |
| Table: | Yes. |
| Group: | But we get the impression that you speak for yourself rather than for the council, that they are advisory only, right? |
| Table: | Yes (enthusiastically). |
| Group: | So the council is there to facilitate the interaction rather than to monitor the interaction, right? |
| Table: | Yes (emphatically). |
| Group: | Are souls sometimes counseled and guided by other souls in preparation for a new lifetime on earth? |
| Table: | Yes. |
| Group: | Is the advisory group present with you at the moment involved in that guidance and preparation process for other souls? |
| Table: | Yes (hesitantly). |
| Group: | Are you yourself involved? |
| Table: | Yes. |

Group: Do you have special experts who determine whether a soul is eligible to be reincarnated?

Table: No.

Group: Do you have special counselors or advisors who help souls decide whether to embark on a lifetime on earth?

Table: Yes.

Group: Are all souls eligible for reincarnation?

Table: Yes (with hesitation).

Group: By hesitating, are you saying that perhaps some souls would need counseling and guidance before embarking on a lifetime on earth, yet this may not be necessarily the case with all souls?

Table: Yes (after considerable hesitation in which the source was apparently consulting with the council).

Group: The others gathered with you are in full accord then with you on this?

Table: Yes.

Group: Generally speaking then, to be or not to be reincarnated is by personal choice?

Table: Yes.

Group: Do souls deliberately select which body they will occupy when embarking on a new lifetime?

Table: Indecisive or cannot answer (indicated by three taps of the table following a long hesitation. Apparently the others present had difficulty reaching consensus on this issue).

Group: Is the selection of a body to occupy at times random?

Table: Yes.

Group: Is the selection at other times more specific?

Table:      Yes.

Group:      Is there always a certain point of prenatal development
            at which embodiment occurs?

Table:      No.

Group:      Is it possible for embodiment to occur at conception?

Table:      Yes, but without consensus of the council (one tap fol-
            lowed by a hesitation and then three taps).

Group:      There seems to be a lack of consensus on this issue,
            right?

Table:      Yes.

Group:      Is that a good thing?

Table:      Yes.

Group:      Then it's acceptable to hold different views, even on im-
            portant things related to the afterlife and reincarnation?

Table:      Yes.

Group:      Are the others who are present with you in agreement
            on this point—that holding different views is okay?

Table:      Yes.

Group:      Is that because holding different views means that we
            are thinking for ourselves, rather than letting others do
            the thinking for us?

Table:      Yes (enthusiastically, with a very strong tap on the
            ground).

Group:      And in that way we each discover what is right for us in-
            dividually?

Table:      Yes.

Group:      It is important, then, to be tolerant of views that differ
            from our own, even on such important matters as rein-
            carnation and the afterlife?

Table:     Yes.

Group:    We can conclude then that diverse opinions and beliefs are acceptable, and in some instances, even desirable.

Table:     Yes.

Group:    And you are sure the council of souls there with you is in full agreement with this?

Table:     Yes (following a pause in which the source was apparently consulting with the council).

Group:    Is it possible for embodiment to occur at birth?

Table:     Yes.

Group:    Does embodiment also occur during the fetal stage of prenatal development?

Table:     Yes.

Group:    In instances of identical multiple births, does embodiment always occur at the same time for each individual?

Table:     No (enthusiastically).

Group:    In instances of conjoined twins, does embodiment always occur at the same time for both individuals?

Table:     No.

Group:    Are there souls on your side who have never been embodied on earth?

Table:     Yes.

Group:    Are they less evolved than souls who have been embodied?

Table:     No.

Group:    Are you saying that many lifetimes on earth do not necessarily indicate a high state of evolvement?

Table:     Yes.

Group:    Are some souls older and wiser than others?

| | |
|---|---|
| Table: | Indecisive or cannot answer. |
| Group: | Let's rephrase this: Are some souls wiser than others? |
| Table: | Yes. |
| Group: | Are some souls older than others? |
| Table: | No. |
| Group: | Sorry, we should have known this since all souls are age-less. |
| Table: | Yes. |
| Group: | Can you select the gender of your next embodiment? |
| Table: | Yes. |
| Group: | Is the selection of gender at times random? |
| Table: | Yes. |
| Group: | Is sexual orientation a function of the selection process, that is, can you choose your sexual orientation before you embark on a new lifetime? |
| Table: | Indecisive or cannot answer. |
| Group: | Is sexual orientation a function of choice? |
| Table: | No, but without consensus of the council. |
| Group: | The council is not in full consensus on this? |
| Table: | Yes. |
| Group: | The differences in views about such issues as sexual orientation, then, also exist in the afterlife realm? |
| Table: | Yes. |
| Group: | Is diversity inherent in the evolution process? |
| Table: | Yes (emphatically). |
| Group: | We should then value our differences in beliefs and orientations without trying to impose them upon others? |
| Table: | Yes (emphatically). |

Group:  Can we together reach a state of oneness with the universe and still view important issues differently?

Table:  Yes (emphatically).

Group:  Are souls ever exactly alike in the way they experience their existence?

Table:  No.

Group:  You seem to be saying that tolerance is critical to the evolution of souls?

Table:  Yes (emphatically).

Group:  Changing the subject here—do souls who have committed criminal acts of violence against others exist in your realm?

Table:  Yes.

Group:  Do they remain criminals in the afterlife?

Table:  No.

Group:  How can that be—is it because of the nature of the transition process?

Table:  Yes, but without consensus of the council.

Group:  Is it also because of their continued evolvement in afterlife?

Table:  Yes.

Group:  Can a soul who committed crimes against humanity in one lifetime be recycled as a benevolent, altruistic soul in another?

Table:  Yes.

Group:  Back to the transition, do we sometimes at death reclaim the peak of our past evolvement within that present lifetime?

Table:  Yes (emphatically).

Group:     But if we went wrong somewhere along the way, does it remain a part of our record of experiences?

Table:     Yes.

Group:     And we have to deal with it, or could we say, resolve it?

Table:     Yes (emphatically).

Group:     If not in your realm, perhaps through another lifetime on earth?

Table:     Yes.

Group:     But it could be accomplished in your realm, perhaps with the help of ministering guides and specialist entities?

Table:     Yes.

Group:     Back to your earlier point—at the transition, am I always restored to my highest peak of past development in a given lifetime, even if it is at a point that I reached in my earliest childhood?

Table:     Yes (following a long hesitation).

Group:     Beyond that point, assuming it came early and I lived well beyond it, am I responsible for what followed?

Table:     Yes (emphatically).

Group:     Was I restored to my earlier peak so that I could more effectively cope with, or take responsibility for, what followed?

Table:     Yes (emphatically).

Group:     Can we assume the council is in agreement with you on this?

Table:     Yes (emphatically).

Group:     If I were the perpetrator of injustice in one life, could I become the victim of injustice in the next?

Table:    Yes.

Group:    That could be one way to evolve, and perhaps resolve Karma.

Table:    Yes.

Group:    To change the subject, are all souls divine?

Table:    Yes.

Group:    As souls, can we be divine and defective at the same time?

Table:    No.

Group:    Without labeling them defective, could we conclude that some souls have evolved very little, or almost none at all?

Table:    Yes.

Group:    Are they as worthy or valuable as souls who have reached a very high state of evolution?

Table:    Yes (emphatically).

Group:    Could you say then that all souls are of equal value though not equally evolved?

Table:    Yes.

Group:    Is the existence of souls from everlasting to everlasting?

Table:    Yes (emphatically).

Group:    That is to say I have no beginning and no ending as a soul?

Table:    Yes (emphatically).

Group:    Is the council in full agreement on this?

Table:    Yes (emphatically).

Group:    In the afterlife, are there authority figures or groups who make decisions for us or in any way control our lives?

Table:    No.

Group:     Highly evolved beings are available to help rather than control?

Table:     Yes.

Group:     Does everyone have a spirit guide?

Table:     Yes.

Group:     Does everyone have a guardian angel?

Table:     Yes (hesitantly).

Group:     You hesitated. Is that because spirit guides and angels are essentially the same, or at least similar?

Table:     Yes (without hesitation).

Group:     Are some of them permanently with us while others are with us only temporarily?

Table:     Yes.

Group:     Some of them visit us based on the situation and our needs?

Table:     Yes.

Group:     Do souls sometimes enter a physical body as so-called "walk-ins" to replace another soul?

Table:     No, but without consensus of the council.

Group:     Are there so-called "earth-bound souls"?

Table:     Indecisive or unable to answer.

Group:     Let's rephrase this question: Do some souls experience difficulty letting go of their past lifetime when they die?

Table:     Yes.

Group:     Are there afterlife guides or teachers to help them along that line?

Table:     Yes.

Group:     Is there a physical universe outside the one we know?

Table:     Yes, but without consensus of the council.

Group:    Is there such a phenomenon as a parallel universe?

Table:    No, but without consensus of the council.

Group:    You are obviously familiar with our dimension as we are yours, because you have lived in ours and we have lived in yours. Do some dimensions exist that we are unfamiliar with?

Table:    Yes (emphatically).

Group:    Do the principles of science, including quantum physics, explain other dimensions of reality and how they function?

Table:    No (without hesitation).

Group:    Are there intelligent life forms elsewhere in the universe?

Table:    Yes (emphatically).

Group:    Is the council in full agreement with you on this issue?

Table:    Yes (emphatically).

Group:    Do these other intelligent life forms exist also in the afterlife?

Table:    Yes.

Group:    Extraterrestrials are therefore souls as we are souls?

Table:    Yes.

Group:    Is it possible that some of us existed as extraterrestrials in a past lifetime?

Table:    Yes.

Group:    Is it possible that some of us will exist as extraterrestrials in a future lifetime?

Table:    Yes.

Group:    Possibly in another universe or other unknown dimension?

Table:    Yes.

Group:    In defining the concept of "good," could we conclude that whatever promotes our own evolvement or that of others is "good"?

Table:    Yes (emphatically).

Group:    It would follow then that evil could be defined as whatever impedes our evolvement or that of others.

Table:    Yes (emphatically).

Group:    Do you and the council consider these definitions of good and evil adequate?

Table:    Yes.

Group:    Is table tipping a good way to interact with your realm?

Table:    Yes.

(**Note:** At this point, the table settled to the ground, as if to signal the end of the interaction. Momentarily, however, the table again tilted and then slowly levitated with all four legs clearing the ground before returning to the tilted position.)

Group:    Is the full council now at the table?

Table:    Yes.

Group:    To manifest your presence and acknowledge the value of this interaction?

Table:    Yes.

With a full moon overhead, the table remained in the tilted position for several moments before slowly settling to the ground, a signal that the interaction was about to end. With the table at rest on the ground, participants at the table expressed their appreciation to the source and the advisory council. The full group then reflected together on the tabling interaction and the information that emerged during the session. As could be expected, members of the group expressed diverse opinions regarding several of the substantive issues that arose during the interaction; but none of them expressed doubt concerning the authenticity of the source and the advisory council.

## Table Tipping Over the Caribbean

A few years ago, I participated in another remarkable table tipping session during a private jet flight over the Caribbean (TR 74).

Others present at the table for the session were the Director of the Parapsychology Research Foundation, the CEO of a major company and his wife, an administrative assistant to the CEO and his wife, and their nineteen-year-old son, a college student.

A remarkable feature of this session was the initial stage of the interaction in which an experienced forerunner emerged to introduce the principal subject of the interaction. An aluminum card table, somewhat smaller and lighter than the standard card table, was used for the session. With four participants, including the CEO and his wife, resting their hands lightly on the table's top, the table promptly tilted. Here's a transcript of the session that followed:

Group:     Thank you for your presence. We appreciate the opportunity of interacting with you through the table. May we invite you to answer our questions with one tap of the table on the floor for "yes," two taps for "no," and three taps for "indecisive or cannot answer"?

Table:     Yes (indicated by one tap).

Group:     First, we would like for you to tell us something about yourself. Do you have a history of life on earth in embodied form?

Table:     No (indicated by two taps).

Group:   Let's be sure we understand: You are a soul who has never been incarnated on Earth?

Table:   Yes.

Group:   Have you lived on another planet?

Table:   No.

Group:   Could we think of you then as a preincarnate?

Table:   Yes (following hesitation).

Group:   We noted you hesitated. Is that because preincarnate implies a future incarnation, which for you is indefinite?

Table:   Yes.

Group:   Is the decision yours to make?

Table:   Yes.

Group:   That's a part of the autonomy of all souls?

Table:   Yes.

Group:   Do some souls who have been embodied on earth become earthbound?

Table:   No.

Group:   Then the concept of being earthbound is a misconception?

Table:   No.

Group:   So earthbound souls do exist?

Table:   Yes.

Group:   Oh, I think we know what you're saying. Some souls during their lifetime on earth become earthbound— that is, they are so involved with earth matters that they become enclosed, out of touch with the spiritual?

Table:   Yes (enthusiastically).

Group:   So "earthbound" applies to incarnates rather than discarnates?

Table:     Yes.

Group:     Thank you for clearing that up for us. Another question: Are there many souls on your side who have never been embodied on earth?

Table:     Yes.

Group:     Are some of them highly evolved?

Table:     Yes.

Group:     Since you have never existed in human body form, could you take on the spirit form of a human body should you decide to materialize and become visible to us?

Table:     Yes.

Group:     Could you take on other spirit forms as well?

Table:     Yes.

Group:     Such as orbs and other forms of light?

Table:     Yes.

Group:     Do you experience emotions similar to those of souls who have lived on earth?

Table:     Yes.

Group:     Does a part of your evolution occur vicariously?

Table:     Yes (enthusiastically).

Group:     That's to say, you grow through empathic participation in the experiences of others, including incarnates.

Table:     Yes (emphatically).

Group:     Have you vicariously experienced human emotions such as sympathy, affection, trust, joy, and tenderness?

Table:     Yes.

Group:     Disappointment, sorrow, dismay—have you experienced emotions like these?

Table:      Yes.

Group:     If you are a personal guide for a soul who experiences these, would you probably experience them vicariously?

Table:      Yes (emphatically).

Group:     Is that one way you learn, by being a spirit guide and sharing the experiences of others?

Table:      Yes.

Group:     We understand that there is great diversity among souls, with no two being exactly alike.

Table:      Yes.

Group:     When souls reach a very high state of evolution, are they more alike?

Table:      No (emphatically).

Group:     More different?

Table:      Yes (emphatically).

Group:     So one of our goals should be to develop our unique potentials, and in doing so, we tend to come into our own, so to speak?

Table:      Yes.

Group:     So is a total oneness of all souls possible?

Table:      Indecisive or cannot answer (after very long hesitation).

Group:     You hesitated. Are you saying that in some ways, there could be a oneness of souls?

Table:      Yes (without hesitation).

Group:     Such as unconditional love for all souls?

Table:      Yes.

Group:     But while real love prevails, we would each still maintain our own individuality and unique makeup.

Table:      Yes.

(**Note:** As the interaction unfolded, participants at the table began to sense that the preincarnate source was present for some purpose other than conveying information about the other side. The pace of the interaction was rapid, not to suggest impatience but the need to move forward to some other objective.)

Group:   Thank you for the invaluable information you have pro-
         vided us, but we feel there may be another purpose for
         your presence.

Table:   Yes (an instant response).

Group:   As we speak, is there someone else there with you?

Table:   Yes.

Group:   And you are there to represent that person?

Table:   Yes (following hesitation).

Group:   You hesitated—was that because you are there to help
         rather than represent?

Table:   Yes.

Group:   As if to introduce that person?

Table:   No response.

Group:   You did not respond—is that because you are consult-
         ing with that person?

Table:   No response.

(**Note:** The table then slowly settled to the floor as the group waited in silence. Finally, the table again tilted, and remained, albeit un-steadily, in the tilted position.)

Group:   Are you a different source?

Table:   Yes (a very slow, unsteady response).

Group:      Thank you for your presence and your willingness to communicate with us. You are familiar with our communication code?

Table:      Yes.

Group:      Is the other source we communicated with still with you?

Table:      Yes.

Group:      To help in the tabling interaction if needed?

Table:      Yes.

Group:      Have you communicated before through the table?

Table:      No.

Group:      The table is just a tool that helps us to interact.

Table:      Yes.

(**Note:** At this stage, the source's responses became more rhythmic and without hesitation.)

Group:      Do you have a special connection to someone in this group?

Table:      Yes (with great enthusiasm).

(**Note:** At this point, an eerie but not uncomfortable silence fell over the group. The CEO then turned to his wife and said, "Could this be R . . .?", a reference to their teenage son who had died almost a year earlier. What followed was a joyful but at times tearful interaction involving father, mother, and son.)

Father:     Is this R . . . ?

Table:      Yes (with obvious excitement and joy).

(**Note:** A period of silence followed in which mother and father experienced an intensely emotional reunion with their son.)

Father:      (tearfully): Are you happy there?

Table:       Yes (without hesitation).

Mother:      (tearfully): We love you and still miss you. I thought I couldn't go on after you left us—I didn't even get to tell you goodbye.

Table:       Yes (compassionately).

Father:      We need to know for certain that you are in a good place...

Table:       Yes (excitedly).

Father:      ...and that you're okay.

Table:       Yes (without hesitation).

Mother:      You crossed over so young—I had trouble accepting that. Was your early crossing meant to be?

Table:       Yes (gently).

Mother:      Was it because....

Table:       Yes. (The answer came before the question could be completed, as if through telepathy.)

Mother:      I know you always loved doing things for others—do you know that your organs went to others as you had wished?

Table:       Yes.

Mother:      Do you sometimes visit us at home?—It's like you are there with us at times.

Table:       Yes.

Mother:      Were you there to let us know you were safe and happy on the other side?

Table:       Yes.

Father:      I know how much you loved scuba diving. Are you still scuba diving?

| | |
|---|---|
| Table: | Yes (excitedly). |
| Father: | I know you loved competitive sports. Do they have them over there? |
| Table: | Yes (excitedly). |
| Father: | But are they still as much fun? |
| Table: | Yes, yes (two single taps with a pause between them). |
| Father: | You said yes and then yes again. Does that mean sports are even more fun over there? |
| Table: | Yes (excitedly). |
| Father: | You told me once that you thought you had been a jaguar in a past life. Were you? |
| Table: | Yes. |
| Father: | Honestly, are there jaguar spirits where you are now? |
| Table: | Yes. |
| Father: | And other animal spirits as well? |
| Table: | Yes. |
| Mother: | You know that we love you as we always did. |

The table then slowly settled to the floor, thus signaling the end of the interaction. A sense of the young man's presence lingered, however, for the remainder of the flight.

For R—'s parents, the table tipping experience provided not only closure for grief but also a new opening for a joyous interaction with their son. For them, their old perception of death as a sad ending was replaced with a new awareness of abundant life beyond.

## Summary

The very nature of death as a transition rather than a termination ensures the possibility of spontaneous as well as deliberate interactions with souls on the other side. Such strategies as Interfacing and table tipping are based on the simple twofold premise that souls survive bodily death and interacting with them can be important to our personal evolvement. More specifically, interactions between the incarnate and discarnate realms are important because:

1. They provide reassurance of life after death. Friends and loved ones who cross over do often contact us to reassure us of their joyous transition. It can be a very dramatic manifestation or simply a comforting inner awareness of their presence.

2. They can satisfy our needs to interact with those who precede us to the other side as well as the needs of the departed to interact with us.

3. They can provide information about the nature of life after death and the opportunities that await us on the other side.

4. They can promote recovery from grief, particularly in instances of sudden or unexpected death.

5. They can add enrichment and meaning to our lives. They can provide a broader view of our existence and increase our understanding of life as forever ongoing.

6. They help us to re-evaluate our life's goals and frame them in ways that encompass the afterlife.

7. They help us to recognize the incomparable value of all souls.

8. They can promote our spiritual growth and motivate us to develop our highest potentials.

9. They can increase our appreciation of all living things.

10. They motivate us to contribute to the greater good.

It's comforting to know that there's a place for everyone in that for-ever endless dimension we call the other side. Rich in new growth opportunities, it awaits our return to bring out the best in us. It's a dimension of abundant love, understanding, and peace. Its breath-taking beauty and wondrous appeal, as we have seen, surpass all physical realities—they pale in comparison to them. It's a place where our highest dreams are realized. It's a realm of eternal reality where each soul finds its noblest expression.

It's an exciting place of freedom, diversity, and challenge, a place to both give and receive. It's a place that welcomes our interaction, a place poised to share its power, knowledge, and enlightenment. It's the perfect place for the continued evolution of souls. It's a realm devoid of hellish forces, punishment, or monster beings—these are the intemperate creations of the imaginative human mind.

As Einstein noted, "The eternal mystery of the world is its com-prehensibility." We could add to that observation, the eternal mys-tery of the spirit world is, likewise, its comprehensibility.

*. . . nearly everyone who tries his powers touches the walls of his being occasionally, and learns about how far to attempt to spring.*
—Charles Dudley Warner, "Third Study," Backlog Studies (1873)

# ASTRAL PROJECTION AND THE AFTERLIFE

Have you ever been abruptly awakened from drowsiness or sleep to experience the jolting sensation of suddenly returning to full wakefulness?

During sleep, have you ever dreamed of flying, perhaps over familiar terrain, and viewing in detail a scene below?

Have you ever awakened from sleep to experience disorientation concerning your location or surroundings? It may have taken awhile for you to get your bearings and to reorient yourself to directions or the layout of your room.

Have you ever experienced during a passive state of relaxation or reverie the sensation of literally leaving your body and traveling to a spatially distant location? In that state, have you actually interacted with others, perhaps engaging in conversation or feeling emotions?

If you've had these experiences, you are not alone! Our surveys showed they are common to almost everyone. They're not illusions or products of the imagination. They each have the unmistakable fingerprint of astral projection.

Astral projection, also known as out-of-body experience (OBE) and soul travel, is a state of being in which consciousness functions apart from the physical body to experience other realities. In that context, consciousness is a function of the astral body, the spiritual counterpart of the biological body. In astral projection, the astral body disengages the physical body while remaining connected to it by the so-called "silver cord," a lifeline that energizes the physical body and sustains it during the out-of-body state. Only at death is the silver cord severed, thereby fully disengaging the spiritual body from the physical.

In the projected state, the astral body as the bearer of consciousness is seemingly unlimited in its capacity to experience other temporal and spiritual realities. Here are a few examples:

- A former student whose grandmother recently moved to a distant city viewed her new premises from overhead during sleep. He noticed a dislodged brick on the walkway leading to her front door. A phone call to his grandmother the next morning proved the accuracy of his out-of-body experience.

- A business owner planning a trip to Cairo visited during sleep the hotel where she would stay. She noticed in the lobby a bright yellow phone and a man behind the desk with his arm in a sling. Upon her arrival at the hotel the next day, each detail of her visit was confirmed.

- A teacher with experience in astral projection traveled out-of-body to visit a colleague who had recently moved from New York to Hawaii. Upon entering the house, she noticed a large arrangement of mixed flowers on a round table in the center of the foyer and a marble sculpture of a woman on the first landing of the staircase. A phone call verified the details of her visit.

- A student who was involved in a serious automobile accident experienced a spontaneous out-of-body state in which he viewed his apparently lifeless body from overhead as it was placed in an ambulance and transported to a hospital. He remained outside his body during emergency surgery which he also viewed from overhead.

- A TV reporter who had been trained in out-of-body travel accepted a new position in a distant city. Prior to relocating, he decided to visit out-of-body the new work setting where a very attractive woman he had not met commanded his attention. Upon reporting for his new work assignment, he instantly recognized the woman who was later to become the love of his life.

As seen from these examples, out-of-body travel can be either spontaneous or deliberately induced. One view of astral projection holds that the out-of-body state is so common that we all experience it spontaneously on a daily basis, particularly during sleep. Dreams of flying or floating in space are believed to be astral travel.

Our case studies found that spontaneous OBEs during sleep often involve interactions with the other side, to include visits with departed relatives or friends (TR 64). In many instances, they provide crucial information of life and death relevance. A building contractor, for instance, reported a dream-like visit with his deceased father the night before an important business trip. In the visit, he was transported as if out-of-body with his father at his side to a certain location on the mountainous road he would travel the next day. As they viewed from above a sharp curve, his father pointed out a huge bolder, tenuously situated just beyond the curve on a high embankment as if poised to fall onto the road below.

With his father's visit still fresh on his mind, he started out early the next day on the trip as planned. Upon approaching the familiar sharp curve as seen with his father the night before, he slowed his car and cautiously rounded the curve. Blocking the road immediately ahead was the huge boulder which had just fallen from the high embankment. According to the contractor, he would have collided with the boulder had he not slowed his car upon approaching the sharp curve. His interaction with his father, he believed, literally saved his life.

Perhaps not surprisingly, among the most effective astral projection strategies known are those that use the sleep state as a vehicle for astral travel. As we've seen, sleep not only promotes spontaneous out-of-body travel to distant temporal destinations, it can connect us to the departed who become our travel companions. Our studies repeatedly suggested that sleep can literally break the communication barrier between dimensions. It can link conscious awareness to the spirit realm and promote direct out-of-body interactions with it.

One very popular view of sleep holds that sleep itself is an out-of-body state, in that during sleep, the astral body disengages the physical to hover gently over it for the duration of sleep. To fall asleep then may literally be to slip out of body. A sudden interruption of sleep that results in a startling awakening could be explained as the abrupt, premature reengagement of the astral with the physical. According to this view, many of our dream experiences, particularly lucid dreams characterized by being borne aloft, are actual out-of-body travel experiences.

Since out-of-body travel seems to spontaneously occur during sleep, it would seem reasonable that controlled strategies designed to utilize the sleep state could facilitate deliberate astral travel to designated destinations, including both temporal and spiritual. It is important to note that the setting for astral travel using any procedure must be safe and free of distractions.

## *Hypnagogic Arrest Strategy*

Whether sleep is an out-of-body state or simply a state conducive to out-of-body travel, strategies that utilize sleep have been highly successful in promoting astral travel. One of the most effective is the Hypnagogic Arrest Strategy which was developed in our laboratory to induce travel during sleep to designated destinations, including the discarnate realm (TR 47). The procedure is designed to arrest the early hypnagogic stage of sleep—that in-between, hypnotic-like state during which the mind is particularly receptive to suggestion. During that arrested state, the simple procedure establishes a mental condition conducive to out-of-body travel during sleep.

This strategy is based on the premise that sleep is a normal altered state in which the astral body as the embodiment of consciousness is receptive to travel to predetermined destinations. Just prior to sleep, the procedure designates a particular location, and then arrests the initial stage of sleep, called hypnagogic, during which astral projection spontaneously occurs. Astral travel to a designated destination then follows. Upon completion of the travel experience, you may spontaneously enter a state of restful sleep during which your astral body remains in its normal projected state, or you may experience a reengagement of the astral with the physical to result in full wakefulness.

It's important to read the entire procedure before starting. The steps are well defined and should be easy to follow. Here's the procedure.

### Step 1. Preliminaries

Before falling asleep, clear your mind of all active thought and, with your eyes closed, formulate your goals of travel, whether into the spirit world or to a distant temporal reality. In setting your goals, be as specific as possible, but do not close your mind to other experiences. Your goal may be simply to experience those spiritual or physical realities that are presently relevant to you. Invite your personal guides to accompany you throughout your astral travel. They will provide protection and empower you to benefit from the experience.

### Step 2. Body Scan

As you prepare to enter peaceful, restful sleep, mentally scan your body and release all tension. While lying preferably on your back with your legs uncrossed and your hands resting to your sides, begin the scan at your forehead, and slowly progress downward, letting relaxation soak deep into the muscles, joints, and tendons of your body, from your head right down through the tips of your toes. Follow up the body scan with peaceful imagery of a special place, such as a tranquil moonlit cove, still meadow, or secluded beach. Immerse yourself in the imagery until drowsiness ensues.

### Step 3. Finger Spread

Upon becoming drowsy, spread the fingers of either hand, and hold them in the spread position. You will feel the tension building in your hand and spreading into your arm. As you remain drowsy, continue to hold the spread position as the tension in your hand builds.

### Step 4. Tension Release

Very slowly relax your fingers as you sense the tension lifting. As your fingers become increasingly relaxed, let relaxation spread over your hand and into your arm. Let the relaxation in your hand and arm then spread slowly over your entire body as you become more and more drowsy.

## Step 5. Astral Projection

With your body now loose and limp and yourself ready to drift into restful sleep, you will sense the gentle release of your astral body from the physical. Allow plenty of time for that projected sense of awareness to unfold. Flow with the experience of being outside your body—do not resist it.

## Step 6. Astral Travel

With your physical body at rest and your astral body disengaged from it, you are now free to travel wherever you decide through sheer intent alone. Restate your goals and affirm your intent to achieve them through out-of-body travel. For travel to the spirit realm, give yourself permission to experience the spiritual dimension and to understand its present relevance in the company of your spirit guides. For travel to spatially distant physical realities, affirm your intent to go there and to benefit from the experience. For unspecified destinations, give yourself permission to spontaneously experience whatever realities are relevant to you. If possible, form a cognitive map of your journey and envision your destination. Be receptive to the visual aids your consciousness provides in cooperation with your personal guides to help focus your travel. Remind yourself that you are safe and secure in the company of your personal guides.

Take time to enjoy the experience! Travel freely and be receptive to the interactions that are enlightening and empowering. Set aside any preconceived notion about astral projection that could become a barrier to productive travel. Your travel experiences will be unique to you. Do not try to fit them into a set of unworkable rules about OBEs.

## Step 7. Astral Return

Upon completing the astral travel experience, give yourself permission to return to your physical body either to immediately re-engage it and thus awaken, or to remain suspended over it until wakefulness and re-engagement occur later on.

## Step 8. Reflection and Resolution

Once you have re-engaged your physical body, take time to reflect on the experience and its relevance. Express your appreciation to your spirit guides who accompanied you in the experience. Relate the astral experience to your present life situation.

## Step 9. Journal

Keep a journal of your OBEs.

A college student who used the Hypnagogic Arrest Strategy to travel out-of-body during sleep reported an interesting visit to the discarnate realm in which he interacted with Albert Einstein. Accompanied by his personal guide, he visited the spirit realm with its many planes and beautiful structures, including a garden-like setting in which Einstein led a group discussion on the nature of multiple dimensions, including the spirit world. Behind Einstein was an expansive concave screen which he filled with complicated formulas and calculations using a laser-like pointer to write on the screen. The student, upon his return, immediately recorded Einstein's conclusions as follows:

> As you can readily see from our calculations, the form of time as we know it in this plane is symptomatically caused by the dominant energy of this plane known as light and can be nonexistent or different on other planes determined by the dominant and subdominant energy forms.

Careful not to divulge any of the related circumstances, I shared the quote with a colleague, a professor of physics, who responded, "That seems like something Albert Einstein would say." As you may recall, it was Einstein who said, "The fairest thing we can experience is the mysterious. It is the fundamental emotion which stands at the cradle of true art and true science. He who knows it not and can no longer feel amazement is as good as dead, a snuffed-out candle."

In a later astral visit to the same setting as before, the student again interacted with Einstein in the garden-like setting. During a discussion of the timeless nature of the afterlife, Einstein confided, "We are all a part of an unending stream of life that has neither beginning nor end."

In researching his astral visits, the student uncovered the following quote from Einstein who, as a young man, was struggling with depression and illness: "I feel myself so much a part of all life that I am not in the least concerned with the beginning or the end of the concrete existence of any particular person in this unending stream."

Another student, a health science major, used sleep intervention to reunite with her deceased husband. Upon entering the spirit realm, she recognized her husband surrounded by spectacular beauty. They embraced and he expressed his deep love for her and their child who was born soon after his sudden death. He called the child by name and pledged to watch over her, as he had since her birth.

In researching the Hypnagogic Arrest Strategy, I decided to use it myself to visit the other side. I entered the out-of-body state with ease and traveled to what seemed to be a festival or celebration of some kind. I was one among many souls, several of whom I recognized and felt a special affinity. Among those who commanded my attention was a classmate who had died soon after graduating from high school. He appeared youthful and full of life as he had before his death. I then recognized an old friend of many years who had recently died of pancreatic cancer in his early seventies. Smiling and glowing in a healthful radiance, he now looked to be at his prime, totally free of the effects of illness and aging. It was a joyous reunion that affirmed my beliefs in death as a gateway to a more abundant life with power to restore souls to their peaks of past growth.

Together, the subjects (including myself) who used the Hypnagogic Arrest Strategy to visit the discarnate realm had experiences consistent with those of our past-life regression subjects as earlier discussed. We, like them, stood in awe at the magnificence of the discarnate realm. We saw planes of color and forms of indescribable beauty. We experienced a serene state of complete balance and attunement. We interacted with departed relatives and friends. We recognized ministering specialists who had guided our growth during our between-lifetimes intervals. We returned with a renewed sense of purpose and direction in our lives.

## Eye Blink Procedure

The second astral projection strategy called Eye Blink Procedure utilizes eye blinks and innovative orientation techniques designed to induce the out-of-body state and facilitate travel to either physical or non-physical destinations (TR 90). The procedure, which is based on the research of Gene Chamberlain of the Parapsychology Research Foundation and tested in our labs, incorporates remote viewing as a practice exercise into a procedure designed to induce astral projection. Astral projection and remote viewing are similar in that they both provide information concerning spatially distant realities. They are different, however, in that astral projection, unlike remote viewing, incorporates disengagement of the astral body from the physical and usually includes a much wider range of experiences. Once you have developed your remote viewing abilities, astral projection is much easier to master.

It is important to read the entire procedure before starting. The steps are well defined and easy to follow. Here's the procedure.

## Step 1. The Setting

Select a safe, quiet area that facilitates walking among a variety of items, such as tables, chairs, sofas, appliances, and plants. The typical home setting with living room, dining room, family room, and kitchen connected provides an excellent situation. If a large area is unavailable, a single room or office with space for walking around furnishings is sufficient. The setting should include a comfortable recliner or couch for use during astral projection. Select the specific path you will follow while walking, preferable a circular route which includes a variety of things to view.

## Step 2. Physically Walking

Walk slowly through the path you selected, paying special attention to what you see on either side.

## Step 3. Viewing and Eye Blink

After walking through your selected area several times, stop and pick a well-defined object, such as a lamp or vase. Gaze at the object for a few seconds and then snap your eyes shut. Rather than closing them slowly, snap them as you would if blinking. Think of taking a snapshot of the item with your eyes. With your eyes closed, you will note that the afterimage of the object will remain briefly. When the image disappears, open your eyes and repeat the exercise. You will note that when you first start this process, the image may turn negative. This will change with practice.

## Step 4. Forming Mental Impressions

As you continue to practice Step 3, you will notice that the afterimage of the selected object stays with you longer. As the duration of the image increases, you will note that a mental impression of the image remains for a few moments even after the image itself fades. Developing this awareness requires practice, possibly for several minutes. Test your effectiveness by turning your head to see if the mental impression remains. When the impression of the image remains, you are ready to go to the next step.

### Step 5. Walking and Eye Blinking

Resume walking around the area you selected as your chosen path. As you continue to walk, repetitively snap your eyes shut for about a second then open them for about a second while always facing forward. Carefully adjust your eye-blink rate and step so as not to stumble or collide with anything. Upon beginning this routine you will probably see the images in your mind's eye as stationary. After several times around and possibly more than one session, you will notice that when your eyes are shut, the items continue to move so that your eyes can be closed longer before the movement stops. You will know you have this mastered when the objects you envisioned are adjacent to you when you open your eyes.

### Step 6. Mentally Walking

Having mastered Step 5, find a comfortable place to recline or lie down with your legs uncrossed and your hands resting at your sides. As you relax, make the entire trip mentally with your eyes closed. While mentally walking through your selected space, pay special attention to the familiar details along your pathway. Observe them from different viewpoints as you sense yourself walking among them.

### Step 7. Remote Viewing

As you remain relaxed with your eyes closed, select a familiar distant place and view it remotely. Pay particular attention to the specific details of the distant setting you are viewing. Take plenty of time for the setting to emerge in full detail.

## Step 8. Astral Projection

Having remotely viewed a distant setting, you are now ready to travel out of body. With your eyes remaining closed, mentally walk around your selected path once more. View in detail the setting as you move among its furnishings. As you continue this mental exercise, you will begin to sense yourself literally walking out-of-body through the room, maneuvering among pieces of furniture and noticing objects in even greater detail. You will then sense that you can travel out-of-body beyond the room to experience firsthand other surroundings, including the place you remotely viewed in Step 7. You are now ready to walk out the door and travel to that place. Take plenty of time to travel to that place, and once there, add to your awareness such sensations as hearing and touch. Remain in that place long enough to get a full sense of your presence there.

## Step 9. Distant Travel

You can now travel to places you have not physically been before. Note your sense of freedom and control. By intent alone, you can travel in any direction to any location you choose. Your destination can include both physical and spiritual realities. You can travel to familiar distant settings or to places totally unknown to you. You can observe others, including other astral travelers, and possibly interact with them. You can engage the spirit realm, again by intent alone. You can interact with your spirit guides and other entities in the spirit realm. You can experience the magnificent beauty of that dimension and the empowerment resources it offers.

## Step 10. The Return

To return to your physical body and re-engage it, give yourself permission to first return to the familiar setting you visited earlier, and from there to your physical body at rest. Allow plenty of time for yourself to slip into your body, fully re-engaging it. When you notice such sensations as breathing, heart rate, and weight, you will know you are back in your body.

### Step 11. Resolution and Verification

Take a few moments to reflect on your out-of-body experiences. Explore the relevance of the experiences, particularly your visitations to the spirit realm. Verify as far as possible that what you experienced during astral travel was accurate.

In a three-phase study conducted in our labs, twenty volunteer subjects used the Eye Blink Procedure to develop their remote viewing and astral projection abilities, though the lines separating these two skills are sometimes blurred (TR 82). Phase I studied the usefulness of the procedure for remote viewing. Phase II studied the procedure's effectiveness as an out-of-body travel strategy. Phase III investigated the capacity of the strategy to induce astral travel to the afterlife realm.

Under controlled conditions, several of our subjects in Phase I were able to use remote viewing to view photographs they had never before viewed, including a volcanic eruption, a cruise ship, and a wooded snow scene. The photographs were placed top side up on a table in a warehouse behind the Parapsychology Research Foundation by a research assistant who was not present for the experiment. Of the twenty subjects participating in the experiment, eleven accurately described the volcanic eruption, thirteen accurately described the cruise ship, and nine accurately identified the wooded snow scene. Eight of our subjects accurately described all three photographs.

In a second phase of the study, all subjects who had participated in the remote viewing phase used the Eye Blink Procedure in an effort to travel astrally to a spatially distant location of their own choosing. All subjects participating in this phase believed they were successful in traveling out-of-body to their selected destination, which they each described in considerable detail.

In the final phase of the study, the twenty subjects were instructed to travel out-of-body to the afterlife realm. They were provided no information concerning the nature of that realm or how they could disengage physical reality to experience it other than the techniques detailed in Step 9 of the Eye Blink Procedure. All subjects participating in this phase reported success in traveling to what they believed was the afterlife realm. They used a variety of strategies to enter that realm, including affirmations, imagery, and even consultations with their spirit guides.

Our subjects' descriptions of the afterlife realm were varied, but with certain common features, all of which were consistent with our past-life studies using EM/RC and the Past-life Corridor. Upon entering the realm, all subjects reported that they stood in amazement at its unparalleled beauty. They were flooded with soft light as they viewed the afterlife stretching out endlessly before them. They felt a natural part of that realm and did not hesitate to engage it. They experienced a "connected oneness to it," a term commonly used by them, and a strong sense of belonging. They freely interacted with other souls, and like our regression subjects, several of them experienced the other side as a "homecoming" in which they were warmly embraced. All souls were seen as attractive beings. Some of our subjects recognized their personal guides as well as acquaintances they had known in this lifetime. Like our regression subjects, our astral travelers experienced a variety of other beautiful energy forms, to include the spirits of animals. Genuine, unconditional love prevailed throughout the spirit realm.

Our astral travelers' descriptions of the structural features of the spirit world were likewise similar to the descriptions of our regression subjects. They saw beautiful planes of color and several of our subjects actually engaged them to experience their empowerment frequencies. One of our subjects interacted with an emerald green plane of shimmering energy which she believed to be healing in nature. Another subject visited a radiant blue plane with frequencies she described as peaceful and serene. These findings are consistent with our previous research which found that astral interaction with spirit planes of color resulted in effects consistent with those color frequencies (see my book *Astral Projection and Psychic Empowerment*).

Some of our subjects visited beautiful gardens with fountains of fluid energy and other exquisitely designed settings in which souls gathered to be enlightened and draw from the growth energy that infused these special places. Nowhere did our subjects experience the domination of superior souls—oneness and equality prevailed. Evil, threat, danger, and oppression were nowhere to be found.

Upon ending their excursion into the afterlife and returning to the physical body, our subjects felt that they brought back with them a new understanding of the afterlife realm. Some of them re-examined their views of death and the afterlife. They concluded that death is a rich transformation after which our growth reaches new peaks of enlightenment and joyous fulfillment.

## Astral Excursion

Throughout this book, I have emphasized *real love* as the most powerful force in the universe. Real love energizes our evolution, ensures our immortality, and enriches our daily existence.

Second in power to real love is *imagination*. As Albert Einstein noted, imagination is more powerful than knowledge. It is imagination that gives rise to knowledge. Where would the world be today without the brilliant imagination of Thomas A. Edison, the Wright brothers, and Henry Ford?

Mental imagery is the brick and mortar of imagination. Through mental imagery, we can build powerful structures within which we can achieve our highest goals. To imagine your goals is the first step in achieving them. It's the picture that's worth a thousand words.

While out-of-body travel is reality, not imagination, the most effective procedures for inducing it use imagery. If you can envision your astral body disengaging your physical body to travel to other locations, you are well on your way toward astral travel. And if you can envision your astral travel destination, you are well on your way toward reaching it. The Astral Excursion is based on this simple twofold premise.

Astral Excursion was designed to promote the highest form of astral travel: out-of-body interactions with higher astral planes (TR 83). Through this procedure, you can actively engage various astral planes and interact with advanced astral entities, including spirit guides, teachers, and other growth facilitators. They are loving, caring beings who await your interaction, constantly poised to accompany you and guide your travels among various planes in the spirit realm.

Before initiating Astral Excursion, it is important to familiarize yourself with the full procedure. Allow approximately one hour for the procedure which is conducted in a quiet, safe, and comfortable setting. Here's the procedure.

### Step 1. Goal Imagery
While resting in a comfortable, reclining or prone position with your legs uncrossed and your arms resting at your side, close your eyes and reflect on your goals. State your goals, both general and specific. If possible, envision your goals as positive realities. For instance, if your goal is to travel among distant cosmic planes and draw energy from them, envision the various planes and yourself engaging and interacting with them.

## Step 2. Physical Relaxation

With your eyes closed for the remainder of the procedure, relax your body by first slowing your breathing and then mentally scanning your body from your head downward, letting all tension go as your body becomes loose and limp. To deepen the relaxed state, envision a scene that is particularly relaxing to you—a tranquil lake, mountains in the distance, a golden meadow, or moonlit landscape, to mention but a few of the possibilities.

## Step 3. Affirmation

With your body now relaxed, affirm your intent to travel out-of-body to interact with the spirit world and to experience its relevance to your stated goals. Affirm the presence of your personal spirit guide as your partner and protector throughout the experience.

## Step 4. Induction

Induce the out-of-body state by first envisioning your physical body at rest. Take plenty of time to form a very clear image of your body at rest, noting your physical characteristics and your fully relaxed state. With the image of your physical body clearly in your mind, sense your astral double as a bright light form rising gently upward from your body and bearing with it your conscious awareness. Note the sense of disengagement and release as you float gently upward. From your out-of-body position, you can again view your body at rest below. Let yourself become fully immersed in the experience of being out of your body.

## Step 5. Astral Engagement

You are now ready to travel to the spirit realm. Re-affirm your intent to explore distant astral realms and engage their powers in the company of your ministering guides. At this point, envision the spirit dimension and give yourself permission to experience it. You will sense yourself actually engaging the spirit realm and becoming a part of it.

## Step 6. Infusion of Love

Upon engaging the spirit world, note the wondrous infusion of cosmic love, the most powerful force in the universe. You cannot engage the spirit world without experiencing it. Infuse yourself with it to empower your total being. Remind yourself that love is the essential element of your spiritual evolution.

## Step 7. Personal Interactions

Joyful reunions with departed friends, relatives, and animals often occur at the state of love infusion, usually in the presence of your personal guide along with other ministering guides. These interactions are invariably empowering for all involved.

## Step 8. Cosmic Plane Interaction

In the company of your ministering guides, you can now interact with the spirit realm's multiple planes of color. Focus your attention upon them, and engage them at will through sheer intent alone. The color of each plane signifies its specialized empowerment properties. For spiritual enlightenment, engage the violet plane; for balance and attunement, engage the blue plane; for mental, physical, and spiritual healing, engage the green plane; for intellectual growth and learning, engage the yellow plane; for your motivational and security needs, engage the orange plane; and for a rapid infusion of energy, engage the red plane. Linger in each plane as long as you need to fully experience its empowering properties.

## Step 9. Return and Re-engagement

To end the excursion experience and return to your physical body, affirm your intent and focus your attention on your physical body at rest in its familiar setting. Intent alone is a sufficient vehicle for ending travel and re-engaging your physical body. Once in the presence of your body, view it again at rest and allow yourself to gently re-enter it. Such physical sensations as tingling, warmth or coolness, weight, and breathing will signal full astral/biological re-engagement.

## Step 10. Resolution and Conclusion

Reflect on the experience and contemplate its empowering effects. Notice your sense of well-being and personal empowerment. Recall your goals as previously stated, and re-affirm the empowering results of your out-of-body travels in your own words. Examples are: *I am at my peak mentally, physically, and spiritually. My life is filled with love and power. I am enveloped in peace and tranquility. I am empowered to achieve my highest goals.* You may wish to conclude the procedure with affirmations of global relevance, again in your own words. Examples are: *I am committed to helping others and making the planet a better place. I will work toward ending hunger, poverty, and disease. I will use my resources to prevent human and animal suffering and abuse.*

In our labs, we incorporated astral travel to the spirit realm in our studies of rejuvenation, health and fitness, and such intellectual functions as memory and problem solving (TR 84, TR 85, TR 86). Our studies found that out-of-body interactions with green cosmic planes seemed to actually slow aging and in some instances reverse its visible effects. Our subjects who bathed in astral pools of shimming green energy were convinced they had been infused with age-defying energy. Patients in our pain management program who used out-of-body techniques to control pain found that interacting with green energy planes not only reduced the intensity of pain but also accelerated healing.

For our subjects who interacted with yellow energy planes, performance on tests of memory and problem solving dramatically

improved. Many of them began using the technique regularly, particularly before exams, to improve their academic performance.
They attributed increases in their grade point averages to the continued use of the procedure, a reflection of the very practical benefits of guided OBEs.

## Summary

Astral projection is one of the most direct ways known for experiencing the spirit world. Through hypnosis and past-life regression,
you can travel inward to retrieve important experiences from out of
your most distant past, including your preexistence, past-lives, and
life-between-lifetimes. Those experiences are stored within yourself
as a part of your evolution as a soul. Through such strategies as Interfacing and table tipping, you can interact with the discarnate
realm as it presently exists.

Through astral projection, you can further extend your search
for new understanding and self-empowerment. You can travel outward to directly experience the spirit world and access its abundant
resources. You can interact with discarnate loved ones, masterful
teachers, and ministering guides. You can bathe in celestial pools of
revitalizing and rejuvenating energy. You can draw multiple powers
from the many planes of color and use them to achieve your highest goals.

Through astral projection along with the other strategies presented in this book, nothing is beyond your reach. If you've ever
dreamt of soaring into the great reaches of the cosmos, you can do
it now. You can discover new meaning to your life in the present
and the magnificent realities that await you in the future. You can
now take that extraordinary leap into the great beyond.

# TECHNICAL REPORTS

TR 2    "Rejuvenation: How to Live Longer and Better," 1964.

TR 3    "The Past-life Corridor Procedure," 1976.

TR 4    "Investigations into Kirlian Photography," 1977. (Funded by U.S. Army)

TR 5    "Eye Movement, Reverse Counting, and Other Induction Procedures," 1976.

TR 7    "Spirit Guides: Their Roles and Functions," 1988.

TR 8    "Case Studies Using EM/RC/Reverse Counting Trance Induction," 1990.

TR 9    "The Kirlian Connection," 1985. (Funded by Parapsychology Foundation, NY)

TR 12    "Hypnosis and Hypnoproduction," 1982.

TR 16    "The Nature of Preexistent Life," 1999.

TR 18    "Preexistence: A Case Study Approach," 2000.

TR 19    "Preexistence and Its Current Relevance," 2001.

TR 20    "Kirlian Photography and Past-life Regression," 1990.

TR 27    "Interfacing: Probing the Afterlife," 1982.

TR 28    "The Legend of Bart," 1987.

TR 31    "Past-life Regression: Interviews with Past-life Regression Subjects," 1997.

TR 33    "Past-life Regression: Interviews with Past-life Hypnotists," 2002.

TR 41    "Rejuvenation: Forever Young," 1999.

TR 42    "The Nature of Spiritual Interaction in Preexistence," 1993.

TR 44    "Life Without Borders: The Preexistence Experience," 1997.

TR 47    "Hypnagogic Arrest Strategy: Procedures and Applications," 1987.

TR 49    "Table Tipping on Founders Green," 1991.

TR 52    "Case Studies: Life-between-lifetimes," 1995.

TR 53    "Life-between-lifetimes and Preexistence: A Comparative Study," 1998.

TR 54    "Life-between-lifetimes: A Self-Discovery Approach," 1998.

TR 55    "The Green Sphere: Exploring Its Healing Properties," 1987.

TR 64    "OBEs: Case Studies," 1995.

TR 66    "Preservation of Peak Growth," 2002.

TR 71    "ESP and Past-life Regression," 1998.

TR 72    "Doors: Strategies for Developing ESP," 2001.

TR 74    "Table Tipping over the Caribbean," 2002.

TR 81    "Interfacing: Real-Life Applications," 1995.

TR 82    "Remote Viewing and Astral Projection," 2003.

TR 83    "Astral Excursion for Self-Empowerment," 1994.

TR 84    "Astral Excursion and Rejuvenation," 1997.

TR 85    "Astral Excursion and Physical Fitness," 1997.

TR 86    "Astral Excursion and Intellectual Functions," 1998.

TR 90    "The Eye Blink Procedure," 2003.

# SUGGESTED READING

Andrews, T. (2002). *How to Uncover Your Past Lives.* St. Paul, MN: Llewellyn Publications.

Bromiley, G. W. (1978). *Historical Theology.* Grand Rapids, MI: William B. Eerdmans Publishing Company.

Cockell, J. (1996). *Past Lives, Future Lives.* New York: Simon & Schuster.

Denning, M. and O. Phillips. (1994). *Astral Projection: The Out-of-Body Experience.* St. Paul, MN: Llewellyn Publications.

Durant, W. (1939). *The Life of Greece.* New York: Simon and Schuster.

Fisher, J. (1984). *The Case for Reincarnation.* New York: Bantam.

Freeman, J. (1986). *The Case for Reincarnation.* Unity Village, MO: Unity Books.

Freedman, D. N. (1992). *The Anchor Bible Dictionary*, Vol. 6, New York: Doubleday.

Head, J. and S. Cranston. (1979). *Reincarnation: The Phoenix Fire Mystery.* New York: Warner Books.

Moody, R. (1991). *Coming Back: A Psychiatrist Explores Past-life Journeys.* New York: Bantam Books.

_____. (1976). *Life After Life.* New York: Bantam Books.

Newton, M. (2000). *Destiny of Souls.* St. Paul, MN: Llewellyn Publications.

_____. (1995). *Journey of Souls.* St. Paul, MN: Llewellyn Publications.

_____. (2004). *Life Between Lives.* St. Paul, MN: Llewellyn Publications.

Paulson, G. (1994). *Meditation and Human Growth: A Practical Manual for Higher Consciousness.* St. Paul, MN: Llewellyn Publications.

Puryear, H. B. (1982). *The Edgar Cayce Primer.* New York: Bantam Books.

Redfield, J. (1996). *The Tenth Insight.* New York: Warner Books.

Rossetti, F. (1992). *Psycho-Regression: A New System for Healing & Personal Growth.* York Beach, ME: Weiser.

Slate, J. (1998). *Astral Projection and Psychic Empowerment: Techniques for Mastering the Out-of-Body Experience.* St Paul, MN: Llewellyn Publications.

_____. (1988). *Psychic Phenomena: New Principles, Techniques and Applications.* Jefferson, NC: McFarland & Co.

_____. (1995). *Psychic Empowerment: A 7-day Plan for Self-Development.* St. Paul, MN: Llewellyn Publications.

_____. (1996). *Psychic Empowerment for Health and Fitness.* St. Paul, MN: Llewellyn Publications.

_____. (2002). *Psychic Vampires: Protection from Energy Predators and Parasites.* St. Paul, MN: Llewellyn Publications.

_____. (2001). *Rejuvenation: Strategies for Living Younger, Longer & Better.* St. Paul, MN: Llewellyn Publications.

_____. (1991). *Self-Empowerment: Strategies for Success.* Bessemer, AL: Colonial Press.

Sutphen, T. (1993). *Blame It On Your Past Lives.* Malibu, CA: Valley of the Sun Publishing.

TenDam, H. (1987). *Exploring Reincarnation.* London: Penguin.

Tompkins, P. and C. Bird. (1989). *The Secret Life of Plants.* New York: Harper & Row.

Webster, R. (2001). *Soul Mates.* St. Paul, MN: Llewellyn Publications.

Weiss, B. (1988). *Many Lives, Many Masters.* New York: Simon & Schuster.

Wilson, C. (1971). *The Occult: A History.* New York: Random House.

# GLOSSARY

**age regression:** A hypnotic state in which the subject experiences past events that occurred in the present lifetime.

**astral excursion:** An out-of-body induction procedure specifically designed to promote astral travel to the spirit realm.

**astral projection:** The experience of being in a location outside the physical body with consciousness intact. Also known as out-of-body experience (OBE), astral travel, and soul travel.

**aura:** The external energy system enveloping all living things. See **human aura**.

**aura photography:** Any procedure that photographs the aura. See **Kirlian photography**.

**authentic love:** A state of pure love, sometimes called *real love.*

**automatic writing:** A strategy in which spontaneous or involuntary writing occurs to bring forth information, typically from the subconscious.

**biological genotype:** The genetic constitution of the physical body, to include dominant and recessive genes. See **cosmic genotype.**

**clairvoyance:** Psychic perception of spatially distant realities. See **extrasensory perception.**

**cosmic genotype:** Each individual's unique spiritual or cosmic makeup which remains unchanged from lifetime to lifetime. Also known as **spiritual genotype.**

**cosmic identity:** The soul's unique **spiritual identity,** which exists in perpetuity. See **cosmic genotype.**

**cosmic language:** The universal language of the spirit realm.

**decline effect:** In aura photography, the decline in brightness of recorded images.

**déjà vu:** A phenomenon in which new events appear familiar or as if they had been previously experienced.

**discarnate manifestation:** Any of a myriad of manifestations of the discarnate realm, to include ghosts and hauntings.

**Doors:** A strategy that emphasizes imagery, choice, and self-determination in acquiring psychic information, particularly of a precognitive nature.

**electrophotography:** See **Kirlian photography.**

**EM/RC procedure:** A trance induction procedure using certain controlled eye movements and reverse counting.

**ESP:** See **extrasensory perception.**

**extrasensory perception (ESP):** Perception occurring independently of sensory mechanisms or processes.

**Eye Blink Procedure:** A procedure that incorporates eye blinks to induce both remote viewing and astral projection.

**human aura:** The human body's external energy field which is believed to be a manifestation of the internal energy system's central core.

**Hypnagogic Arrest Strategy:** A procedure that uses the hypnagogic stage of sleep to induce out-of-body travel.

**hypnoproduction:** A trance state in which totally new, highly developed skills emerge.

**hypnosis:** A trance state in which receptivity to suggestion is heightened.

**hypnotherapy:** The use of hypnosis for therapeutic purposes.

**incarnate preparation:** A process of preparation in the spirit realm for embodiment on the earth plane.

**Interfacing:** A group procedure designed to merge the physical realm with the spiritual.

**Karma:** In general, the force generated by a person's actions.

**Kirlian photography:** An electrophotographic procedure designed to photograph the electromagnetic field enveloping all living things.

**life-before-life:** One's existence before one's first incarnation. See **preexistence.**

**life-between-lifetimes:** One's existence in the spirit realm between one's lifetimes on earth.

**life-between-lifetimes regression:** A trance state in which one experiences one's existence in the spirit realm between lifetimes.

**OBE:** See **astral projection.**

**out-of-body experience (OBE):** See **astral projection.**

**oversoul:** The collective life force of souls.

**parapsychology:** A field of study concerned with the study of extrasensory perception, psychokinesis, and other unexplained or paranormal phenomena.

**Past-life Corridor:** A strategy used to explore one's past life, including preexistence, past lifetimes, and life-between-lifetimes.

**past-life illumination:** An increase in the brightness of aura images obtained photographically during past-life regression.

**past-life journal:** A written record of one's past-life experiences.

**past-life regression:** A trance state in which one experiences aspects of one's past life, which can include past lifetimes, preexistence, and life-between-lifetimes.

**Past-Lifetime Chart:** A chart formulated to determine the number of past lifetimes one has lived.

**precognition:** ESP of future events.

**preexistence:** One's existence before one's first embodiment on earth.

**preexistence regression:** Regression to one's existence prior to one's first embodiment.

**preservation of peak growth:** A phenomenon in which one's past peak of development is regained at death.

**psychokinesis (PK):** The ability to influence objects, events, and processes in the absence of intervening physical energy or intermediary instrumentation.

**remote image phenomena:** In aura photography, an image occurring outside the normal range of aura activity.

**remote viewing:** The psychical viewing of a spatially distant reality.

**séance:** A group procedure requiring a medium who communicates with the spirit world.

**secular worldview:** A view of reality that emphasizes the secular over the spiritual.

**self-hypnosis:** The self-induced trance state in which receptivity to one's own suggestions is heightened.

**silver cord:** The support mechanism connecting the physical body to its astral counterpart during astral projection.

**soul span:** The capacity of the soul to span many lifetimes in the evolution process.

**soul travel:** See **astral projection.**

**spiritual genotype:** See **cosmic genotype.**

**spiritual worldview:** A view of reality that emphasizes the spiritual over the secular.

**subconscious:** The vast inner region of experiences not available to conscious awareness. It is believed to be the repository of all past-life experiences.

**table kinesics:** In table tipping, the significance of various table movements, including tipping, vibrations, and full table levitation.

**table tipping:** A group procedure that uses a table as an intermediary device to engage and interact with the spirit realm.

**telepathy:** Mind-to-mind communication.

**trance psychic:** A psychic who engages the trance state during readings.

# INDEX

# LLEWELLYN ORDERING INFORMATION

## Order Online:
Visit our website at www.llewellyn.com, select your books, and order them on our secure server.

## Order by Phone:
- Call toll-free within the U.S. at 1-877-NEW-WRLD (1-877-639-9753). Call toll-free within Canada at 1-866-NEW-WRLD (1-866-639-9753)
- We accept VISA, MasterCard, and American Express

## Order by Mail:
Send the full price of your order (MN residents add 7% sales tax) in U.S. funds, plus postage & handling to:

**Llewellyn Worldwide**
**2143 Wooddale Drive, Dept. 0-7387-0714-7**
**Woodbury, Minnesota 55125-2989, U.S.A.**

## Postage & Handling:

**Standard** (U.S., Mexico, & Canada). If your order is:
$49.99 and under, add $3.00
$50.00 and over, FREE STANDARD SHIPPING

AK, HI, PR: $15.00 for one book plus $1.00 for each additional book.

**International Orders** (airmail only):
$16.00 for one book plus $3.00 for each additional book

*Orders are processed within 2 business days.*
*Please allow for normal shipping time. Postage and handling rates subject to change.*

## Aura Energy for Health, Healing & Balance

### JOE H. SLATE, PH.D.

Imagine an advanced energy/information system that contains the chronicle of your life—past, present, and future. By referring to it, you could discover exciting new dimensions to your existence. You could uncover important resources for new insights, growth, and power.

You possess such a system right now. It is your personal aura. In his latest book, Dr. Joe H. Slate illustrates how each one of us has the power to see the aura, interpret it, and fine-tune it to promote mental, physical, and spiritual well-being. College students have used his techniques to raise their grade-point averages, gain admission to graduate programs, and eventually get the jobs they want. Now you can use his aura empowerment program to initiate an exciting new spiral of growth in all areas of your life.

**1-56718-637-8, 288 pp., 6 x 9**                                        **$12.95**

## Psychic Vampires
### *Protection from Energy Predators & Parasites*

### JOE H. SLATE, PH.D.

Is somebody sucking your life-force energy?

Consuming energy instead of blood, psychic vampires come in a variety of unsuspecting guises. In this unique approach to the subject, you will be introduced to a trio of new thieves: (1) group vampires—organized efforts of predator corporations and institutions; (2) parasitic vampires—an inner vampire state that feeds on your internal energy resources; and (3) global vampirism—widespread conditions that erode the human potential for growth and progress.

Exploring environmental, developmental, and past-life factors, *Psychic Vampires* incorporates practical, step-by-step empowerment procedures that anyone can use to protect themselves and replenish their own energy reserves.

0-7387-0191-2, 288 pp., 6 x 9, illus.                                    $14.95

## Rejuvenation
### *Strategies for Living Younger, Longer & Better*

### JOE H. SLATE, PH.D.

Includes a CD with meditations and exercises from the 7-Day Plan.

Preventing mutations that cause illness, keeping artery walls open and free of blockage, and prolonging the ability of cells to reproduce are reasonable expectations for anyone willing to develop his or her capacity for rejuvenation and longevity. Whatever your current age, you possess the built-in potential to repair and recreate yourself. This book offers 45 new rejuvenation strategies, many of which were developed in a college laboratory setting.

By protecting and fortifying your innermost energy system, you can slow the aging process and even reverse its effects in some instances. Aging factors are flexible and responsive to deliberate intervention. When you turbocharge your inner age-defying mechanisms, you can slow the winged chariot of time and live a longer, richer life.

**1-56718-633-5, 240-pp., 6 x 9 book and meditation CD**          **$19.95**

# How to Uncover Your Past Lives

## TED ANDREWS

Knowledge of your past lives can be extremely rewarding. It can assist you in opening to new depths within your own psychological makeup. It can provide greater insight into present circumstances with loved ones, career and health. It is also a lot of fun.

Now Ted Andrews shares with you nine different techniques that you can use to access your past lives. Between techniques, Andrews discusses issues such as karma—and how it is expressed in your present life; the source of past life information, soul mates and twin souls, proving past lives, the mysteries of birth and death, animals and reincarnation, abortion and premature death, and the role of reincarnation in Christianity.

To explore your past lives, you need only use one or more of the techniques offered. Complete instructions are provided for a safe and easy regression. Learn to dowse to pinpoint the years and places of your lives with great accuracy, make your own self-hypnosis tape, attune to the incoming child during pregnancy, use the tarot and the cabala in past life meditations, keep a past life journal, and more.

0-87542-022-2, 240 pp., illus.                                    **$5.99**

# Journey of Souls
## *Case Studies of Life Between Lives*

### MICHAEL NEWTON, PH.D.

This remarkable book uncovers—for the first time—the mystery of life in the spirit world after death on earth. Dr. Michael Newton, a hypnotherapist in private practice, has developed his own hypnosis technique to reach his subjects' hidden memories of the hereafter. The narrative is woven as a progressive travel log around the accounts of twenty-nine people who were placed in a state of super-consciousness. While in deep hypnosis, these subjects describe what has happened to them between their former reincarnations on earth. They reveal graphic details about how it feels to die, who meets us right after death, what the spirit world is really like, where we go and what we do as souls, and why we choose to come back in certain bodies.

After reading Journey of Souls, you will acquire a better understanding of the immortality of the human soul. Plus, you will meet day-to-day personal challenges with a greater sense of purpose as you begin to understand the reasons behind events in your own life.

1-56718-485-5, 288 pp., 6 x 9                                   $14.95

**To order, call 1-877-NEW-WRLD**
Prices subject to change without notice

## To Write to the Author

If you wish to contact the author or would like more information about this book, please write to the author in care of Llewellyn Worldwide and we will forward your request. Both the author and publisher appreciate hearing from you and learning of your enjoyment of this book and how it has helped you. Llewellyn Worldwide cannot guarantee that every letter written to the author can be answered, but all will be forwarded. Please write to:

Joe H. Slate, Ph.D.
℅ Llewellyn Worldwide
2143 Wooddale Drive, Dept. 0-7387-0714-7
Woodbury, Minnesota 55125-2989, U.S.A.

Please enclose a self-addressed stamped envelope for reply,
or $1.00 to cover costs. If outside U.S.A., enclose
international postal reply coupon.

Many of Llewellyn's authors have websites with additional information and resources. For more information, please visit our website at:

www.llewellyn.com